mission
VENTURED

dynamic stories across
a challenging world

vivienne stacey

D1555873

Inter-Varsity Press

£1-50

INTER-VARSITY PRESS
38 De Montfort Street, Leicester LE1 7GP, England
Email: ivp@uccf.org.uk
Website: www.ivpbooks.com

First published 2001

British Library Cataloguing in Publication Data
A catalogue record for this book is available from the British Library.

ISBN 0–85111–546–2

Set in Garamond
Typeset in Great Britain
Printed and bound in Great Britain by Omnia Books Ltd, Glasgow

Inter-Varsity Press is the publishing division of the Universities and Colleges Christian Fellowship (formerly the Inter-Varsity Fellowship), a student movement linking Christian Unions in universities and colleges throughout Great Britain, and a member movement of the International Fellowship of Evangelical Students. For more information about local and national activities write to UCCF, 38 De Montfort Street, Leicester LE1 7GP, email@uccf.org.uk, or visit the UCCF website at www.uccf.org.uk.

Contents

Foreword

I have waited for the publication of this book for a long time. Why is it important? First, it seems to me there is a lack of written accounts of contemporary models of women God has used in student ministry over the last fifty years in the remarkable history of IFES. These testimonies go some way towards meeting that need. Secondly, the book highlights the roles women have played in pioneering student ministries in different parts of the world. Here you will find stories of courage, faithfulness, persistence and fruitfulness in recent decades. I believe that some of the testimonies will prove inspirational to contemporary generations of students whom I hope will be provoked to exclaim, 'If God could use these women, then surely he could use me!'

The book simply seeks to bear testimony to those whom our sovereign God has seen fit to use in the expansion of gospel ministry among students in a wonderful way in the last five decades. We thank God for them and pray that he will raise up many more. My prayer is that many women (and men) will follow their examples and go and do likewise!

Lindsay Brown
General Secretary
International Fellowship of Evangelical Students

Preface

I wish to express my thanks to Lindsay Brown for suggesting this book at a small meeting in Cairo in 1997 and for his gracious encouragement along the way.

I am most grateful to each of the seven women who have contributed to the book.

I also wish to thank my friends and former colleague, Phyllis Tring, for her many helpful suggestions about the manuscript.

Colin Duriez, the General Books Editor of IVP, has also given me help and advice, for which I thank him.

Paphos, 2001   *Vivienne Stacey*

Introduction

I have placed my own story first so that I can introduce you to the other seven contributors whom I have met in my travels round the world over the last forty years. We come from five different continents and from various religious and social backgrounds. I asked them to write about their early years and educational opportunities, about their journeys into faith and how God guided them to work across cultures. Each has described her pilgrimage. I also requested that each write something on why she married or remained single, so obviously there is a variety of very personal views.

I marvel at the diversity of their experiences. What do these eight women have in common? I think it is that God met with each of us, called us and for many years of our lives gave us unique opportunities to live and work in cross-cultural situations. Some of us still live outside the countries in which we were born. Ada Lum and I know all these women, and each of them knows some of the others.

Probably such accounts of the lives and work of women could only come from the last half century. No other century has accorded women so much freedom to travel and to interact. It remains to be seen how women as well as men will meet the increasing opportunities of the twenty-first century, in which there is likely to be more mixing of ethnic groups, cultures and beliefs. It would seem that Christians have travelled further afield in the first and twentieth centuries, and that those centuries have also witnessed more persecution and martyrdoms than any other. The twenty-first century may witness a renewal of the church which will draw in women and men who will fulfil Christ's manifesto to the church to share the good news with the whole world, starting at any place. The Christian pilgrim, like Abraham, is always moving, whether across the street or across the world, looking forward to the heavenly city 'whose architect and builder is God' (Heb. 11:10). In compiling this book – in fact in all of my writings – I like to think that my friends of other faiths and of no faith are looking over my shoulder. I hope that students and graduates, men and women, people of other faiths and philosophies, as well as Christians, will read this book. Much history has been written by men, so maybe the frank recording of eight women's lives will be refreshing.

Chapter 1

Vivienne Stacey

University

The Second World War had just ended. I was too young to qualify for Oxford or Cambridge, which at that time both required students to be at least eighteen, so I gained admission to University College, London, popularly known as 'the godless institution of Gower Street'. Even in the early part of the nineteenth century, only Anglicans could study at Oxford and Cambridge. Rationalists, of whom Jeremy Bentham was the most famous, started the first college of London University in 1827, declaring in its charter that theology should never be taught and that there should be no college chapel. In October 1945, when I went up to college, only 10% of us were straight from schools. The rest were ex-service people, mostly men, who worked hard all the time and were very serious. University College maintained strong rationalist and communist influences both among students and staff, as I discovered when I explored what various student societies had on offer. One of our lecturers was a communist. It was not a private matter.

Conversion

Barbara, one of my friends in the English department, was a Christian. Before coming to college she had prayed that she would meet someone to whom she could introduce her Lord Jesus Christ. She decided I was that person. Barbara had soon realized that I was not likely to respond positively to an invitation to church. After a few weeks I asked her where she disappeared to every lunch time. To my astonishment she told me that she attended a prayer meeting run by students in the chapel of the neighbouring medical college. It was her turn to be astonished when I said I would like to come along, not to pray but to see what happened. I noticed the sincerity of this small group of students in their praying but could not understand how God (if there was one) could be interested in the small matters that they seemed to be concerned with. I thanked my friend and did not go to another prayer meeting until I joined them as a believer some months later. I was not at peace with myself and was aware that Barbara had an inner happiness that I lacked. Outward morality did not satisfy me. My thoughts and attitudes fell short of my own standards.

In February 1946 Barbara invited me to a Christian youth meeting at the Royal Albert Hall. I declined to take a ticket but said that if I and my friend Betty Stops were out of the theatre in time we would come. Betty was a friend from my schooldays. We came. The first speaker, Dr Martyn Lloyd-Jones, spoke on the raising of Jairus's daughter. He quoted Luke 8:52–53, 'Jesus said, "She is not dead but asleep." They laughed at him, knowing that she was dead.' They, in fact, laughed Jesus to scorn. I immediately realized that this was my position. I was searching for something that would make sense of life. I had thoughts about many things but had no centre to my thinking. I had not even considered Jesus. I had dismissed him as not relevant to the modern world. I had indeed been so dismissive that I had scorned him. The next speaker talked about the resurrection of Jesus from the dead, and I realized that if he rose from the dead he is alive now and can be encountered.

A couple of evenings later as I was studying in my father's office I switched off the light and knelt down. In that instant I had a vision of Jesus. There was light in the room and he was standing ahead of me. I knew that he had died for my sins. His peace flooded my heart. The risen Christ met me in my need. This encounter changed the whole course of my life. I have no regrets, only gratitude to him. Life has been far richer than I ever expected.

The next day Barbara must have noticed a difference in me as she gave me a New Testament. I was puzzled as it was not my birthday, nor was it Christmas. I thanked her and decided to read it every day in the train. Soon after that I joined the small group of students in their regular Bible study and prayers. This was the Christian Union of the Inter-Varsity Fellowship (IVF)[1] to which Barbara belonged. Those early experiences of group Bible study gave me a valuable foundation on which to build, as well as a model for future ministry. In the IVF the students themselves took decisions and ran the programmes, which included prayer meetings, Bible studies and evangelistic activities. They received guidance and advice from visiting field staff called travelling secretaries, but in essence it was a student-led movement. In 1947 the IVF became one of the ten founding members of the International Fellowship of Evangelical Students (IFES), with which I have had so much contact over the years. I started to attend church on Sunday mornings and got permission from our parents to take my ten-year-old brother to Sunday school. After my baptism in 1947 my parents decided to start attending church. Some years later my mother became a believer, and finally so did my father.

Family background and early childhood

My father was a Londoner, the youngest of six children. He was born in 1894, just soon enough to remember a little of Victorian England with its horse-drawn traffic. He grew up in the East End, where his father, from Somerset in south-west England, had made good as a cabinet-maker. Having left school at fourteen, he went to evening classes to improve his education. For some years he worked in a garage and then took up accountancy. He tried to enlist but was pronounced medically unfit for military service in the First World War. For a number of years he worked for a City firm of accountants and then joined the administrative staff of Imperial College, London. In his early thirties he met my mother while they were both on holiday. She was from south Wales and had trained as a schoolteacher. They married in 1927 and set up home in Greenford, Middlesex, a new suburb of London.

I was born on 12 July 1928. About three years later we moved to a semi-detached house in Ruislip, a few miles further out of London. The Underground train line had just been built to reach Ruislip and beyond, and so people started to move out to the suburbs. Our country lane eventually became a main road. My brother, Gareth, was born in 1936. Our parents had very high moral standards and simple tastes. My mother had reacted against her Presbyterian background and my father became a lapsed Anglican, so we had a secular upbringing. However, Gareth was baptized in the nine-hundred-year-old village church, when I had one of few experiences of being taken to church.

Schooling

I was sent to school first for about six weeks in south Wales, where my maternal grandmother lived. I well remember the children wearing national costume and daffodils for St David's Day. My teacher knew my uncle and aunt and did not hold me too accountable for defacing a book and a few other mild misdemeanours. At the age of six I was enrolled in a Church of England primary school in Ruislip. I remember tormenting the vicar, who could not keep order. I enjoyed walking the mile between home and school and playing on the way, as I was often in trouble in both places. I soon got myself expelled from my dancing class. I learned a lot from my high spirits and punishable escapades that proved an enormous help when I myself became a teacher.

My parents had few friends and did little entertaining, but Mr Meyer, a Venezuelan, and his German wife visited my parents each year and they invited us to their home. In the 1930s they had long discussions and many forebodings about Hitler and his rise to power. At each six-monthly visit they always discussed 'the nightmare years'. Although I was very young I still remember the sense of foreboding that these adults had, although then I did not understand it.

The Second World War broke out when I was eleven. After experiencing some of the bombing and blitzing of London in 1940 our mother decided to take my brother and me to greater safety in Wales, while our father continued his accountancy and fire-watching in central London and visited us periodically. I can recall the fall of France and the chill that this news seemed to bring. We went to mid-Wales where my grandmother had moved to escape bombing. I hated my new school, Brecon County School. I was very resentful at having to leave my previous school, which I liked.

After six months we moved to a very old cottage with walls three feet thick, without electricity and water inside. This holiday cottage in the fishing village of New Quay, west Wales, belonged to a first cousin of my mother. In this Welsh-speaking area I went to school by bus, in a town seven miles away. In every school I attended we seemed to study *A Midsummer Night's Dream*, and I became allergic to it for a while; my French also was adversely affected by changes of school. Our English teacher, Mr Meredith, however, was young, tall, dark and handsome. He soon joined the Navy, serving in a submarine which was torpedoed. I never forgot him and his tragic death.

I felt a foreigner in Welsh-speaking Wales. School prayers were in Welsh and nearly everyone talked in the language. At school a small group of us were known as 'the evacuees'. I went to a Welsh Sunday school where the answer to every question seemed to be 'faith' – something I did not have. I developed a great dislike of Welsh nonconformity. Everyone went to chapel, so I soon stopped going. For some years my only interest in visiting churches was to study the architecture.

After I matriculated at the age of fifteen we moved back to England. Our mother took a job as headmistress of a village school in Oxfordshire so that we could live nearer London, as things seemed safe and it was so much nearer for our father to visit every six weeks or so. I went to a school nearby and studied English, Latin, French and history for two years in the sixth form. I remember a very nice family called Prue who lived in the village. The older son, Maurice, went off in the Army and was killed in the jungles of Burma.

After a year our mother gave up teaching and we moved to a village in Northamptonshire that was still near my school. I enjoyed life in the sixth form and here became friendly with Betty Stops. We cycled to Stratford-on-Avon to see plays. Both of us decided to read English at London University. My first cousin, Victor, was shot down flying over Libya. When I was very small I used to watch him march past in his Scout troop.

As the war was ending we got news of concentration camps. By then I was seventeen and began to realize even more of the horror of war. It was not just that I knew a sailor, a soldier and an airman who had been killed.

Call to work abroad

A few weeks after my conversion Barbara, my university friend, invited me to another meeting at which a missionary, Mary Macdonald, spoke briefly about how God had called her to work among lepers in India. I was perturbed that she had studied English, the subject I was studying, as I realized that he might also ask me to work among lepers, and I was unwilling. I left the meeting knowing that God had called me to work abroad. Another verse from Luke confirmed it for me: 'From everyone who has been given much, much will be demanded; and from the one who has been entrusted with much, much more will be asked' (Luke 12:48). I knew God had given me much – new life in Christ and the benefits of a good education.

For a while I struggled, but when I told God I was willing to do what Mary was going to do, I found that he did not require this from me, but he wanted my willingness. My initial focus was now on India because of Mary. The next year India became independent and Pakistan was created in the name of Islam. I had Muslim and Hindu friends in the college and I knew that it was hard to influence Muslims. Somehow this drew me to Muslims and I recognized God's calling to the Muslim world. I wanted to see what the living God would do for Muslims. I continued to collect information and to learn something about Pakistan and Central Asia. I learned about some missionary societies that worked in those areas.

The next question was what career I should follow. I wanted to be a writer. I was able to talk with a well-known Christian writer who had worked in China. She advised me to write articles and booklets but not to try to earn my living as a writer. My mother had warned me against teaching. I did not really know if I had any gift for teaching or not. So I decided to apply to Cambridge and London to do a postgraduate diploma in education. I asked God to guide through these two applications.

I lost my papers for Cambridge, but was accepted at the Institute of Education of London University. I discovered that I liked teaching. I prayed for a teaching post that would be good preparation for work abroad.

Preparation for work abroad

There followed three years in which I taught English and religious education in Cheshire. I was keen to teach religious education, as, since an Education Act in 1944, it became compulsory in state schools and I knew there was a shortage of teachers. I had the conviction that I should use my intellect as much for my faith as for my BA, so I had already taken some evening classes at the London Bible College and had started learning New Testament Greek. My predecessor in this teaching post was a Methodist lay preacher. People expected me to follow in her footsteps, and I started to receive invitations to preach in Methodist, Baptist and Congregationalist churches in nearby towns and in the villages around. I found it a change from teaching children. I cycled to the various locations within a ten-mile radius, and solved the problem of cooking as I was given generous hospitality.

I realized that I needed to do some more formal study of the Bible and Christian theology. The result was that I applied to the London Bible College and was able to do an external BD degree of the University of London. This proved very helpful to me when I eventually lectured in theological seminaries and colleges in many parts of the world. God guided me to apply to the Zenana Bible and Medical Mission, which later became the Bible and Medical Missionary Fellowship, and latterly Inter-serve.

I had reservations about joining a mission which for nearly a hundred years had been a women's mission. However, it had recently received Jack Dain as its General Secretary and Alan

Norrish as its Field Secretary. It had a new policy of co-operation with other Christian agencies and was seeking staff for union theological colleges at the time I applied.

My other reservation was that it was a 'faith mission'. I realized that God had provided for its needs for a hundred years since its foundation in 1852 to work in India in hospitals and schools and among Hindu and Muslim women hidden away in the women's quarters of their houses. I concluded that God would supply for the next century, although few applicants now had private incomes.

I asked to be sent to wherever in Pakistan there was a training establishment to help Pakistani Christian women in their witness among Muslims. Jack Dain told there was only one such place – the United Bible Training Centre in Gujranwala. So I said, 'Please send me there.'

'We like an open offer,' he replied.

'I make an open offer,' I rejoined, 'but please send me there.'

After a year of Urdu study I was sent to the UBTC. I was commissioned by the Ruislip Baptist Church in September 1954 as their first missionary. John Doble, then in his first pastorate, preached from the book of Ruth 1:16, 'Your people will be my people.' My parents, brother and about thirty people from the church and mission came to see me off at Euston Station, London, on the boat train to Liverpool on 2 October 1954. To the surprise of passers-by they made a circle around me, prayed and sang hymns until the train was about to leave.

Voyage to Pakistan, Urdu and orientation

I sailed on *RMS Cilicia*, one of the Anchor Line passenger boats. The voyage took eighteen days. We stopped at Gibraltar, sailed past Cyprus, and called at Port Said and Aden, before reaching Karachi. The ZBMM had requested Mrs Allen, whose family had been connected with India for generations, mainly through the Army and education, to take me under her wing. We sat at the First Officer's table. Mrs Allen was celebrating her fortieth voyage to India and her eightieth birthday. She was a brilliant sharer of the good news of Christ. I learned much from her gracious attitudes and her natural conversations about God. Evangelism was a way of life for her.

In Karachi I said goodbye to Mrs Allen, as she was going on to Bombay. I stayed in Karachi for several days as trains were delayed by floods. A Scottish nurse and a Member of the National Assembly (MNA) were my companions on the lengthy journey to Lahore. I had a long discussion with the MNA, one of the few women members, on the Trinity. I was the sixth ZBMM member to arrive in Pakistan. After a few days in Lahore with future colleagues, I was escorted to Gujranwala by Dorothy Boswell. I remember looking out of the window of the train as we approached Gujranwala and wondering how long I would live there. After a year of language study in Sialkot and Murree it was to be twenty years before the Lord led me out to another part of Pakistan and to a different ministry which took me to every continent.

I enjoyed being a language student for a year. Living with Americans was a new experience as I had had no acquaintance with Americans before. My fellow language student, Gene, and I are still close friends. I doubt if we would have ever got to know each other if we had not been thrown together in the beginning. We lived in an old colonial house with thirty-two outside doors – quite a problem when we had to check security if a thief was around.

One mission interviewer in the UK had grave doubts about my suitability for work in places where learning a language was essential. She had taken me to church and realized how unmusical I was. However, I found that if you put your tongue in the right place and controlled the amount of breath used with consonants, the sounds generally came out right. I learned about the customs and culture from my very gracious senior missionaries and from my students. I had never heard of culture shock and had little idea of what Pakistan would be like. I knew that my senior missionary was studying my reaction to the many flies that settled on the food stalls as we had made a brief stop on our way to Sialkot, where I was to study Urdu for the winter.

On my first leave from Pakistan in 1959 I certainly experienced reversed culture shock. I couldn't bring myself to buy clothes or shoes which had visible labels on them, or zip-up trousers! I was unable to guide foreigners about how to fill in a Post Office form and I had forgotten how to use a self-service restaurant.

Twenty years at the United Bible Training Centre in the Punjab, 1955–75

I took up my post at the United Bible Training Centre, Gujranwala, in September 1955. The UBTC is an autonomous institution with a Governing Board made up of representatives of the main Protestant denominations in Pakistan and a few mission organizations. The Centre trains Pakistani Christian women to work with the church and tries to help them to be more effective disciples in their respective spheres in society. A two-year course was run to train evangelists and Bible teachers until 1966.

One such evangelist was Esther John, who grew up in a Muslim home in India. Through seeing the love of God lived out in her teacher, and through Scripture lessons at her Christian school, she had became a believer in Jesus as Saviour and Lord. She sailed with her family from Madras to Karachi in 1947 to become a citizen of the new country created in the name of Islam – Pakistan. A Christian teacher in Karachi occasionally called at her home and talked with her. When her marriage was arranged with a man who did not share her faith she decided to seek refuge with Christians. Eventually she was baptized and helped to fulfil her calling. She came to the UBTC in 1957. Everyone loved her. We used to go together to visit homes in the villages around. She would speak of her experience of Christ and I would also give a little teaching from the Bible. She graduated in 1959 and went to work in another part of the country. I remember that she and a fellow student called Martha came to intercept me on the train as I travelled to Karachi for my first home leave. I thought how wonderful it was to have such fellow workers and I looked forward to the future.

While I was on leave in the UK Martha wrote to tell me that our sister Esther had gone to heaven. She had been murdered one night as she slept. It was February 1960 and she was thirty years old. The police officer who investigated the case said, 'This girl was in love with your Christ.'

In Britain, during the summer of 1998, ten empty niches over the West entrance of Westminster Abbey, London, the nation's most visited church, were filled with the statues of ten contemporary martyrs. The twentieth century saw more Christian martyrs than any other century. The niches had stood empty since the Abbey was built in the eleventh century. The statues were unveiled during the Lambeth Conference of Anglican bishops led by the Archbishop of Canterbury. One of the ten was that of Esther John. She was the first martyr I had known, but by no means the last.

Munir was a contemporary of Esther doing the same course at the UBTC. After qualifying as a teacher, Munir came to the UBTC. After graduation she worked as an evangelist in a Christian hospital and then as a Bible teacher in a Christian high school. She later joined the staff of the UBTC and served for a number of years before marrying a pastor. With her husband she is now engaged in outreach to tribal people as well as teaching the local congregation in one of the more difficult areas of Pakistan.

Through the years a three-year part-time course for the wives of theological students has continued. From 1966 the Centre put a greater stress on short courses. For one month a year, a course was offered for nurses to help them in their study of the Bible, understanding of Islam and witness to Muslims. Another month's course was held for girls who had just matriculated and were waiting for examination results. They came from all over the country to get a better grounding in their faith and a greater understanding of their Muslim neighbours and friends. Another course was run for teachers, especially to help those who had the opportunity of teaching Christian education in schools. Refresher courses for the wives of pastors, Sunday-school teachers' training weekends and a variety of other courses were offered with the aim of helping women to be lively and effective Christians in whatever situation they found themselves. The UBTC was called a Centre because students came to it, but also because staff could be sent out from it as requested, to run courses in hospitals, schools or church communities. This was the extension service.

In 1966 I became Acting Principal of the UBTC and soon after that Principal. Besides teaching and administration, my work involved some responsibility for building programmes and involvement in various church-related and mission committees. I was one of the founding members of Theological Education by Extension in Pakistan. I taught classes in Gujranwala and Lahore and wrote a workbook on the Old Testament. For fifteen years I was on the Board and Executive Committee of the International Assistance Mission and made about thirty visits to Afghanistan.

Relocation to Bannu in the North West Frontier Province, 1976–91

In 1969 I had asked the UBTC and Interserve for six weeks' leave to visit four of the Arabian Gulf oil countries. I had realized that over half the nurses trained in the United Christian Hospital in Lahore took jobs in Kuwait, Bahrain, the Trucial States,[2] the Sultanate of Oman, Saudi Arabia, Qatar and Libya. I wanted to have a clearer understanding of the situations in which Pakistani Christians were working in the oil countries. I did not realize that God was starting to call me to another ministry and that I would eventually leave the UBTC in 1975. Each year I travelled to the Gulf in the vacations. Then out of the blue in 1974 David Penman,[3] Regional Secretary of IFES, asked me to join his pioneer team for the Middle East, North Africa and the Gulf. I set aside a week to reflect and pray, and concluded that God was calling me to continue to follow the Pakistani Christians in their dispersion, to work part-time with the IFES and to start writing for publication some of what I had been teaching over the previous twenty years at the UBTC. I wrote a proposal for Interserve which included my job description, how it might be financed and where in Pakistan I might relocate. When I submitted it to the Interserve leadership, Jack Dain wrote back that my proposal was in the 'spirit of the Lausanne Congress' which had just taken place. I left the UBTC in 1975 and returned to Pakistan the following year to live in Bannu in the North West Frontier Province with the invitation and blessing of all those concerned. Bannu had not been on my list of possibilities, but Dr Ruth Coggan, who had invited me there for my Christmas 'retreat', continued praying for me to know the Lord's will and made the original suggestion. Bannu proved to be an ideal fellowship base for me.

Following the Pakistani dispersions to the Middle East

In some ways I had been very vague or visionary. I had no idea how a call to the Muslim world would work out or how and where God would lead me. I had known that Pakistan was where to start, in the UBTC. Nearly twenty years later, when Jock Anderson told me that my reports on the Gulf would lead to Interservers working there, I had not ever dreamed of it. It was in the late 1980s that I realized that God had given me a worldwide ministry in training trainers, especially in the Third World, and in challenging and informing, especially in countries of revival, renewal and missionary vision such as South Korea, India and Brazil. My writing ministry meant that materials and information to back this up could go into other languages. God led me into many things that were not on my agenda. Until 1974 I had no idea that I would spend fifteen years in a small fundamentalist frontier town of Pakistan near to the Afghan border.

I began as a missionary from the West; I became a missionary from the East and I ended up a world Christian. Certainly my first visit to Kuwait, Bahrain, the Trucial States and the Sultanate of Oman in 1969 helped me in training nurses and teachers who took jobs in those lands. I returned again to learn more and to teach small groups in the countries I visited. Many of them were very isolated. However, in Bahrain an Urdu congregation had started in 1967. I began to realize something of the significance of Saudi Arabia as the religious and pilgrimage centre of the Muslim world, and of Egypt as the intellectual centre with its influence spread through the Gulf lands by Egyptian oil workers and engineers, and medical and teaching personnel. Pakistan became an Islamic experiment in statehood. I felt compelled to consider the tie-up of economics and religion. I took a fresh look at the Bible to see how God had used dispersions of peoples to further his purposes; dispersions through political oppression as in the case of the Babylonians, and through economic pressure as in the case of the patriarchs in Egypt. The dispersion for trade and commerce of Jews all around the Mediterranean Sea in the intertestamental period seemed to parallel in some respects the dispersions from many lands of people involved in oil production, with the building of infrastructures as the Landrover replaced the camel, and as cities grew in the desert. Religious persecution and mission initiatives were other ways of dispersion, as we see from the Acts of the Apostles. Now there are dispersions into lands where Christians can be employed and also spread the gospel. Gradually I began to relate this to what was happening in the oil lands, which in general had no indigenous churches.

All this opened another world dimension to the sharing of faith. It became an urgent subject for theological, economic, geographical and strategic study. Coming to the Gulf from the East rather than the West coloured my perspective. Having seen the influx of tens of thousands of skilled, semiliterate and illiterate workers from Pakistan, India (especially Kerala) and Bangladesh, I asked a British university economist who lectured and wrote about the Gulf what the prognosis was for the next ten years. He told me that there would be the 'Far Eastern connection' as Koreans and Filipinos arrived. I went to Korea in 1973 to suggest some preparation for the large numbers of Christians who eventually went to the Middle East. Maybe there were ways that they, like the Christians from the Indian subcontinent, might learn that God is Lord of oil and of dispersions. Maybe they would ask with the psalmist, 'How can we sing the songs of the LORD while in a foreign land?' (Ps. 137:4). God gave me visions of his glory active in the Sultanate of Oman and in some of the most unlikely places of the Middle East and Central Asia.

Pioneering with the IFES in the Middle East, North Africa and the Gulf

IFES is a unique fellowship. I have been immensely enriched by the interaction between people of so many nationalities from each continent. It was a refreshing change from some of the western-dominated organizations that I have known. The 'ethos' of IFES is to help in the formation of national student movements as most appropriate for that particular country. My association with IVF and IFES has been lifelong, starting in my student days in 1946. I had been an associate part-time staff worker of IFES for the Middle East and North Africa from 1976 to 1993. I continued to be linked in an advisory capacity until 1996. I have always valued my contacts with IFES. In Pakistan I was a Board member of the Pakistan Fellowship of Evangelical Students for several years (1980–90). I had contacts with many movements through my itinerant ministry.

My first tour for IFES was across North Africa. I kept a watching brief in Morocco, Algeria and Tunisia until I found someone to take on that area – Donna Smith, who speaks fluent Arabic and French. The next assignment was a survey of Iran in 1976, with a view to placing a youth worker, mainly for students. I visited seven university towns and talked to educational and church leaders. Soon afterwards IFES seconded a Pakistani, John Ray, to work under Bishop Dehqani Tafti as a diocesan youth worker based in Isfahan. Subsequently I visited him several times until he had to leave Iran after the Ayatollah's rise to power. I visited Ankara and Istanbul in Turkey, and Syria, Jordan and Lebanon. I found it was easy to get into Lebanon during the civil war if one applied for a visa in Pakistan. I visited each of the Gulf oil states, with the exception of Iraq, and Libya at least three times. I was disappointed to have to refuse an invitation to Sulaimaniya in northern Iraq because it did not fulfil my safety guidelines for travelling alone. With the increasing oil revenues new universities and colleges started to appear in Saudi Arabia and the UAE. Bahrain soon had a university, and the Sultanate of Oman opened Sultan Qaboos University in 1986. There were no Christian students in most of these universities. Early on, most of the suitably qualified staff came from abroad. I kept IFES informed about these job opportunities as new universities and colleges opened.

In the late 1970s and early 1980s we ran Arab student conferences in Cyprus until it seemed better to link north African Christians with the French Groupes Bibliques Universitaires, and Egypt started hosting student conferences for Syrians, Jordanians and Lebanese as well as Egyptians.

In 1993 I had a particularly encouraging three weeks in India. This time I worked in the south in the Bangalore area. The Indian Evangelical Mission (IEM) looked after me very nicely at their rural Outreach Training Institute where I gave forty-one lectures. One student came from the Friends Mission Prayer Band (FMPB). A Japanese couple from the Overseas Missionary Fellowship (OMF) attended, and some other Indians from the north-east of the country, as well as the majority who were from south India. It was exciting to see something of the enthusiasm of indigenous missions. The IEM had 400 workers and the FMPB 500 at that time. Visiting local mosques was a new experience for many of those I taught, and they were surprised by their cordial reception in four out of five mosques. India has over a hundred million Muslims – the largest minority in any country in the world – about 12% of the population. The other highlights of my visit were times with the Union of Evangelical Students of India (UESI).

Writing

I was determined to succeed as a writer in my own culture before I wrote for Pakistan and other lands. After the publication of a few booklets and two books by the Bible and Medical Missionary Fellowship, Concordia Press published my book *Go and Tell: A Case for Christian Mission Today*.[4] So then I started to write for the Christian Publishing House in Lahore, Pakistan. The Pakistani church at that time had fewer than 200 titles in Urdu. Now that I had jumped the barrier and got published in the UK, I thought it was very important to increase the numbers of Christian books in Pakistan, though the editions would be much smaller than in the West. The need was so much greater in Pakistan.

My writing has been in four areas. First, I wrote material to help people to relate to Muslims *Submitting to God: Introducing Islam*[5] and *Women in Islam*[6] are examples. Secondly, I wrote materials related to the history and growth of the Pakistani church, notably a biography of Henry Martyn which was published in Pakistan in Urdu and in India in English, as part of the jubilee celebrations of the Henry Martyn Institute in Hyderabad. It was later translated into Hindi and Marathi. *Thomas Valpy French, First Bishop of Lahore* was another biography, published in Urdu, about a man who was a very gracious sharer of good news. Thirdly, *Bible Studies for Enquirers and New Believers* (Urdu in 1992 and English in 1994) was designed for Muslims. The fourth area was unexpected as far as I was concerned. Through my efforts at learning Punjabi by immersion in Punjabi villages I had come in contact with folk religion and the occult. There was no book in Urdu on this subject. After some years I knew that God wanted me to write on this subject, and so I wrote *Christ Supreme over Satan: Spiritual Warfare, Folk Religion and the Occult*, which was published in Urdu in 1984 and in English in 1986.

Some of my articles appeared in about twenty languages including Korean, Kannada, Urdu, Dutch and English. From time to time I have written strategy papers as well as leaflets for special occasions. Some of my lectures have been videoed and I have also been involved in an English programme on the occult on Dutch TV for Europe.

The excellent professional studio at Columbia International University in South Carolina, USA, recorded for distance learning forty-six half-hour sessions of my course on *Women in Islam* in June 1998. Twenty-three audiocassettes together with a handbook of supplementary materials were prepared for use worldwide, either for credit for an MA course in cross-cultural studies or for personal use under the arrangements of the Muslim Studies Department of CIU. I continue to write articles, booklets and books in these four areas.

Retirement from Interserve in 1993 and church recommissioning

The transition to retirement from Interserve was easy and smooth. I continued to do the things I liked doing and had less committee responsibility. I was a freer agent, just accountable to two churches. God clearly guided me about the next five years (1994 to 1998 inclusive). With the prayers and support of Ruislip Baptist Church and Bishop Hannington Church in Hove, England (where my brother and sister-in-law are members), and the encouragement of many others, I planned to continue writing, itinerant teaching and training of leaders who are keen to reach out and train others for work among Muslims. I took things at a slightly slower pace and put a greater emphasis on writing. I continued to live in my home in Paphos, on the Mediterranean island of Cyprus, to which I had moved in 1991. I am now on my second five-year plan (1999 to 2003 inclusive).

I have seen many changes in Interserve over the years and the way it has developed and grown under good leadership and God's blessing. Nearly a year after I retired from Interserve my friends, Bishop Jack Dain and his wife Hester, wrote on 24 November 1994, 'Last week we attended memorable Interserve meetings at All Souls, Langham Place, London ... Twenty candidates and returning partners were commissioned and we realized what enormous changes have taken place since Jack became General Secretary in 1947. At that time there were forty-five women missionaries working in India and Pakistan. Today the Fellowship numbers over four hundred partners, including men and women from several countries in Asia. They are at work in twenty-six countries from Mongolia through Asia to the Middle East and North Africa in a wide spectrum of specialized ministries but all aiming to make Christ known by deeds and by words.' I have witnessed all these changes and been a part of some of them.

I am deeply indebted to many who have prayed for me over the years, including one member of the church at Ruislip who prayed for me every day from when I sailed in 1954 until her death at the age of ninety-one in 1998. Then there was Elizabeth (Elsie) Waugh, a missionary colleague, who out of the blue sent me £25 many years ago to help me in my writing, for which I needed books. She prayed through the years until her death at ninety-one in 1998. Some of my brother Gareth's Cambridge friends joined in praying and contributing towards my support from 1960 until now. I know that others still pray for me daily, including my Pakistani student, colleague and friend, Munir. There are many others who pray regularly. I will never know what I owe to the prayers of others.

I have experienced the kindness of God and answers to prayers especially in health matters. When I first had attacks of malaria, which troubled me for years, I rationalized that as I didn't die the first time, I supposed that I would be OK the next time. Those were the days of quinine injections. I was quite ill in 1964 with rheumatic fever. The Lord assured me that I would be completely healed. A friend prayed to that end using the words from Isaiah 53:5, 'by his wounds we are healed'. I had two years of sick leave in the UK in 1964 to 1966. I still remember being told by my doctor, a Harley Street specialist, 'Go and rest for six months.' After that was completed he told me, 'Go and rest for a year.' I never lost the sense that the Lord was healing me and that I would be able to return to Pakistan. I learned to get around using buses and taxis and I was allowed to walk a mile on the flat every day. I discovered a new way of reading – read for an hour and rest for an hour. It improved reflection and I received many ideas for future writings. When I was quite ill in 1995 as a result of a possible complication from diabetes I asked God to give me fifteen more years of life (for writing), as he did to King Hezekiah.

I have experienced remarkable safety in travel. I once began to think that for planes to touch the landing strip and then go up again immediately was normal procedure until I enquired about it from a Christian leader who did more travelling than I. In a ministry that often involved physical and spiritual risk-taking I have always felt that the safest place is in the centre of the will of God. Sometimes I have been scared. Several of us visited Afghanistan in 1980 after the murder of two Finnish colleagues. There seemed to be a pall of fear over the city. God met us in our need and we were able to bring counsel and encouragement into a difficult situation.

'Why aren't you married?'

In 1 Corinthians 7:7 St Paul writes about the gift of celibacy. In the 1946 meeting in the Albert Hall one speaker mentioned that in serving God some might take a lonely road and not marry. I had a vague sense that this might apply to me. For years I did not embrace celibacy as positively as I might have done. I learned to thank God for being single in that I could not have maintained a lifestyle of thirty years of constant travel – travelling about six months of the year – and never being in one place longer than a couple of months, were I not single. As it was, I was able to travel at short notice if necessary. I developed a fairly strong conviction that I would never marry, but I did not rule it out. I never renounced marriage but I never sought it. Now I very much enjoy being single.

I once had a conversation with an Arab student who was on standby for terrorist activities in the Middle East. He was studying in an Indian university but always on call. We were guests in the same Christian home. He asked me what my work was, so I told him I was a writer. Naturally he asked what I wrote about, so I showed him what I had written that morning for a Bible study on St Paul's letter to the Romans. We had a short Bible study together, after which he said, 'Do you mind if I ask you a question? Why aren't you married?'

'Before I answer you may I ask you a question?' I replied. 'Why aren't you married?'

He replied, ' I am on special assignment.'

'So am I,' I said.

He understood perfectly. Later through the love of God he experienced in that home, he became a follower of Jesus and sought a new way of life in yet another country, seeking to share the good news about Jesus.

In the following chapters, I will introduce to you some of my IFES colleagues. Some married when they were young, one later in life, and the rest remained single. The question was not marriage or singleness, but what is God's will. We are all still on pilgrimage trying to follow and obey our Lord until we come to the city of God (Rev. 21:2).

Chapter 2

Gladys Peter

Background of the Union of Evangelical Students of India

As early as 1949 an active group of staunchly evangelical students in Calcutta was holding regular prayer meetings. Norton Sterrett was appointed by IFES to work in India. In July 1951 the Madras Inter-Collegiate Christian Union was formed. By 1954 members from several groups met for a retreat near Katpadi and the Union of Evangelical Students of India was born. The new movement was criticized for its reliance on the Bible as the inspired word of God. Lest it be accused of depending on foreign finance, it adopted a policy of mainly indigenous support. In 1956 P. T. Chandapilla, a gifted and austere figure, became the movement's first Indian staff worker. He continued with UESI for twenty years until he left to become the General Secretary of the Federation of Evangelical Churches in India. The first All-India Camp was held in 1957. After that camp work sprang up in many parts of India. The Indian student movement was affiliated to IFES in 1959 as the

Union of Evangelical Students of India (UESI). Thirteen of India's twenty-one states had at least one group by 1964. A Graduates Fellowship emerged after a conference in 1962.[1]

Vivienne introduces Gladys

I first came in contact with the UESI when I was requested to run seminars in Lucknow and Hyderabad for their staff on ministry among Muslims and understanding Islam. I met Shadrach Peter at the Hyderabad seminar in the early 1980s. Later in the 1990s when the IEM and UESI twice invited me to Bangalore for the same sort of work, I met Shadrach's wife, Gladys (née Charles), and their four children. Twice I had the privilege of staying in their hospitable home in Bangalore, Karnataka State, South India. The Muslims of India are easily met. It troubled me that although the Indian church was lively and growing and the UESI was reaching nominal Christians and Hindus, Muslims were not high on the agenda. By 1999 there were 15,000 Indian missionaries belonging to 300 Indian missionary societies, but only about 1% worked among Muslims.[2] I found that Gladys as well as Shadrach shared my vision for reaching Muslim students and the Muslim communities in India. They also had great concern for the students from abroad who came to study in India, many of them Muslims from Iran and further afield.

During my two visits to Hyderabad I was the guest of Shadrach and Gladys for about three weeks in all. I got to know their children and to admire the way they supported each other especially in illness and disability. I appreciated their open home where individual students felt so welcome.

I was impressed by their simple lifestyle. Travelling to meetings on the back of Shadrach's motorbike was not my favourite occupation, but I saw how God protected us in the traffic hazards. Gladys combined her responsibilities as wife, mother and hostess with her local student work, and from time to time travelled to various parts of the state, or even further afield to camps and conferences. I was glad when she had the opportunity to take a course in London at the Institute for Contemporary Christianity, founded by John Stott. I admired the way the family was able to grieve together when their daughter Sweety died at the age of thirteen. In joy and grief, through hardship and under pressure, Gladys gave us all an example of a Christian sustained by the power of God's indwelling Spirit.

Gladys writes her own story

On a hot summer day with temperatures around forty degrees in Madras (recently renamed Chennai), my friend and I sat for the forty-minute train journey to visit a militant Hindu college where a girl had invited us. We were fortunate to get seats. I opened my notebook, going through the notes for the Bible study at the college, but my thoughts ran on. 'Is it worth going all this way in the hot sun for one girl? And what if the college authorities catch us reading the Bible on the campus?' I wiped the sweat off my face, and closed off the negative thought. 'It is worth it, even for one girl only. We will meet her.'

I was a twenty-year-old staff worker with the Union of Evangelical Students of India, and I was getting the message, 'God cares', even for one individual. My youth let me easily pass as a student, and as the girl and I sat under a tree to read, the authorities did not notice.

I had learnt early in life that God cares about individuals. It started with my mother. When my grandmother died of the plague in the 1920s, my grandfather, knowing he could not care for his three daughters, walked for about three days to take them to a Methodist Mission Hostel and leave them in the care of a lady missionary. My mother, one of these girls, learnt later that her father too died in the plague. Spared from death, mother grew up in a school and became a teacher herself. Her name was Ruth, my father was Charles, and I was born on 10 April 1948.

We lived, ate and slept in a one-room house with no running water, electricity or toilet, but I did not notice the lack for years. My days filled up with play, friends, school, and basking in my parents' love for their only child. They had less love between each other.

My father had much of his button manufacturing business in what became Pakistan and, in the troubles of 1947 at independence and the partition of India, he lost most of it. My mother supported the home with her teaching, but there was no harmony. I remember often hiding in fear in the corner when my father beat my mother. I feared his anger would fall on me. It did, the day I lost my slate when I was in standard 1 at the nearby school. I told my father at lunch time that it was lost. Fury broke lose. 'You are so careless,' he screamed, taking a cane and coming after me.

I ran distracted on my five year-old legs. 'I have committed some shocking crime,' I concluded. 'Where can I go?' My short legs took me back up the road to school. I looked back and saw that he was still chasing me. I ran even faster. My teacher, a Catholic nun, calmed me, heard my story, and recovered the slate from my seat-mate, who had stolen it. I dreaded my father's anger as long as he lived.

Raichur, on the dry, dusty plateau between Bangalore and Bombay, has summer temperatures from forty to forty-five degrees. When we could not bear to sleep in the house, we put a bedspread outside the front door and lay in the sweltering darkness. My father was a Christian only in name, but one night lying there he told the story of the woman at the well who drew water and gave a drink to Jesus. I liked the story, but Jesus did not seem real.

I was afraid of the dark if I was alone. At the Catholic school I learnt to make the sign of the cross, and made it once as I was going home from a friend's place after dark. An old Catholic lady said, 'You are Protestants. This is our sign.'

My friends made up my life. With a group of girls I laughed and played through all circumstances. We often enjoyed boys' games and played with two pointed sticks and marbles as well as hide and seek. School work was easy for me. The headmistress reduced my school fees because I was from a poor home. I enjoyed examination times, studying with wealthy friends in their huge bungalows with electric fans and rich food. They used to give me treats if I showed them my answer sheet in class tests. With friends I never felt alone, but I also learnt to tell lies, pinch the other girls, and take things from other people. This was my life philosophy. You pinch people to get your own way. You grab anything you need like pencils, erasers, clothes and bangles. My closest friends did this to me too.

Occasionally we travelled five hours by bus to Hyderabad. I dreamt about that city where my mother's relatives gave me ice-cream, food of the privileged. When my parents sent me there to do my pre-university course it seemed like a dream come true, a place of frivolity and enjoyment. At fifteen I thought I was on the road to the pinnacle of success.

People saw me as a Christian because in India your name often tells your religious group, and I was Gladys Charles. Christians tried to get me to come to their group, but I disdainfully dodged them. The cousin with whose family I boarded, and who seemed considerate of me, invited me to meetings at the nearby Methodist Church, and also to the Evangelical Union. The first time they got me to go to an EU camp, I was struck by what I heard. 'They say Jesus touches lives,' I thought to myself. 'Is this true?' I kept thinking it over.

One evening an Australian missionary asked me, 'Do you have Jesus in your heart?'

'No,' I answered.

'Do you want Jesus to come into your life?' That question offered me life.

'Yes.' I felt ushered into the home of a heavenly Father, a place I had avoided for so long. My journey in Christ began.

Christian life has a lot to do with friendship. The love and caring of Christian friends buoyed me up and made me feel wanted and recognized in spite of all the undesirable things I knew were in me. Here I was, a small-town, inconspicuous newcomer to the big city, but because I was a Christian I made good.

My first Bible was borrowed. I started slowly, taking the EU advice on how to study it and then how to lead small Bible study groups. Soon they asked me to lead a small group myself. In that secular atmosphere it became obvious to others that I was a Christian. In my college campus I used to teach for half an hour only one girl. I think that's where I learnt so deeply the value of even one person.

Just three months after I accepted Christ, there was a jolt to my life. My father, who loved me very much, passed away. I had only my mother to cling to, as I was an only child. But I learnt an important truth. I now had a heavenly Father, even when my earthly father was gone. I felt truly comforted. The pain that could have made me bitter gave me a deeper knowledge of Jesus. As a Christian I belonged to a large family. I took seriously Jesus' words in Matthew 12:50, 'For whoever does the will of my Father in heaven is my brother and sister and mother.' I was learning to love others and also receive love.

The Methodist Church in Hyderabad, its godly pastor, and the Sunday school and youth fellowship impressed me. The American pastor and his wife cared so much that I realized that in Christ being an American or Indian makes no difference. Christian love breaks down barriers. With their care my spiritual life grew. Any time I had a question about what I read in my daily Bible study, or a question when I talked to my friends about Jesus, I took it to my pastor and his wife. I owe a lot to them. They motivated me as a new believer in Christ to keep moving on.

Can I get the balance right?

I was studying for a BSc in botany, zoology and chemistry and at the same time studying German and English, but in my new intensely Christian environment, my academic pursuits took second place. I was young and zealous. I realized I was making an impact on the lives of young Christian girls as I encouraged and discipled them. I don't think I realized then how much I was investing in younger people, but even today I see the results in changed lives. The gospel can change selfish people into self-giving, caring people. I still passed my exams.

I wondered if, since Jesus touched me with his love as a young college student, I could do the same for others by giving my life to serve Christ. Just when I was about to finish my BSc, a telegram arrived inviting me to take up a post as a science teacher in a Christian high school. I thought hard, weighing up my earlier feeling that God was calling me in a different direction and the need for further Bible study. I declined the offer.

Dr Norton Sterrett and his wife had started the Asian Bible Study Centre under the Union of Evangelical Students of India (UESI) further south in the cool hills at Kotagiri, offering an eight-month Bible course for lay people. I wanted to go there, rather than start teaching, but I had no money for fees.

When they gave me a free place to study there I took my first steps in the UESI principle of trusting God for all financial needs. I learned literally to look to God for my every need. If God could send ravens to feed his servant Elijah, he could also take care of me. I received assistance for my fees and every other need. The difference was that the ravens were in human form.

My Hyderabad pastor and his wife gave me my first woollen sweater, white with pearl-like buttons, and a woollen blanket for the cooler climate. I was astounded. Many people I was close to had exploited me, so I had continued my philosophy of grabbing. Now someone had given. The old philosophy had to be changed. I wanted to learn to give. Those eight months at Highfield in Kotagiri made a lasting impact on me. I enjoyed acquiring biblical knowledge, but what stands out today are the lessons at the dining table, on the sports ground, in free time, and in kitchen duties. I saw Dr and Mrs Sterrett teach the Bible and then scrub cooking pots or clean toilets. In our Indian system this is a detestable job. Slowly I learnt to look at all jobs as right and good when done for the sake of Christ.

The ten of us at this Study Centre included a Nepali girl, a Filipino couple, a Malayali from Kerala, a Timilian, a Telugu, a Naga from north-east India, and a Kannadiga from Karnataka. Our backgrounds and temperaments were poles apart and so were those of our visiting teachers. Yet we could live harmoniously. More, we became like a family. That was another lesson for life.

I was nineteen years old, full of life and zeal for helping women students entering higher levels of education. Especially in our culture, they needed women Christian workers. UESI earlier had a few western women workers, and in 1967 appointed its first two Indian women, but then one left to get married. Rita Jackson was alone, and women were not encouraged to travel alone. I longed to help. I prayed, 'Is this the right task for me?' One of the senior staff wrote, 'Perhaps you are too young to join as staff.' Discouraged, I returned to Raichur. 'Anyway,' I reasoned, 'my mother is alone since my father died. Perhaps God wants me to work here in a secular job to be near her.'

At the same time UESI leaders must have realized that the women's work would go back to square one when Rita could not travel alone. They wrote inviting me to join UESI so that they could also train me for the future. But my mind was full of questions. 'Perhaps I should stay with my mother and teach in Raichur. We're so poor I should help her. I should seek a government job with security and a pension at the finish. How would I survive if I worked for UESI with no fixed income? How would I feel, leaving home permanently to live far away in Madras? Besides, by custom a girl my age should be thinking about marriage, not being an itinerant Christian worker. People hardly think that a decent occupation for a Christian girl.'

A friend from Hyderabad stayed with me for three days in Raichur to give me much-needed encouragement. We talked, prayed and asked God to let me know his will. A verse that Dr Sterrett quoted to me kept coming back, 'And who knows but that you have come to royal position for such a time as this?' (Est. 4:14). The words challenged me. The incipient women's work could flounder while the position of women in my country was still precarious. I started to feel that this was the right move for me, but the biggest hurdle was still leaving my mother behind. As I expected, she said 'No', and in Indian thinking I was still answerable to my parents and would have to obey her.

I prayed again for guidance. Words from Matthew 10:37 seemed made for me. 'Anyone who loves father or mother more than me is not worthy of me.' Asking Jesus to give me grace as I said it, I told my mother, 'I must go. I follow Christ.' Hesitantly she finally gave her permission. I booked my train ticket and got my things ready. Mother wept as we said goodbye at Raichur station. She was letting go her best possession. No wonder it upset her. With the bravery of youth, I felt tough and unmoved as I farewelled her, bolstered by another Bible verse, 'Those who honour me, I will honour' (1 Sam. 2:30). I felt I had held God's honour higher than tender human affection, and he would not let me down.

Youthful staff worker

In huge cosmopolitan Madras I still felt my small-town background. Languages and cultures from all over India met in that city where we two women staff workers were supposed to reach across the country. At twenty I had all the energy in the world. Nothing was too difficult for God. I would be a brave soldier for Christ.

Talking to college girls about Jesus came naturally. I look back on myself at that time and I think I was 'intoxicated with Jesus'. I would not stop sharing the good news about Jesus with anybody – in trains, buses, at bus stops, in auto rickshaws. I still do. I told how Jesus answered all life's problems. I was so young I could get close to the other girls. I visited colleges back and forth across Madras, meeting girls during their free time or lunch break, talking with individuals and conducting Bible studies.

Rita and I made trips out of Madras, learning to travel light. It was fun seeing the country. Often I visited a hostel to talk to or counsel a girl and stayed in her hostel room sleeping on a mat on the floor. A friend reminded me recently that I gave her advice about marriage though I was unmarried myself. I loved the work. I could see Jesus changing lives as I taught about him.

Then came the inevitable crisis. It is rare to stay single in India. Rita was to marry and leave UESI. What would they decide now about me as a single woman? I supposed the leaders would think I was afraid to continue alone, but somehow I felt stronger than ever before. I believe that was from God. The General Secretary, whom I respected, asked, 'What will you do now you will be left alone?'

Taking my courage in my hands, I responded, 'Please don't close the women's department. I'm still here.' The department continued and God gradually brought more women with vision and courage to reach out to young women in India.

I was working on the need myself, learning to recognize the young women with potential to mentor and encouraging them to join the staff. We travelled less, but met daily to pray for girls by name, some from different parts of India, some who wrote to us whom we never met. In answer, we heard how young women could keep their stand as Christians in harsh situations and difficult homes. The family of UESI was for me, an only child, a new and warm experience. Staff heartened one another, interacted and supported. I learnt how we could be brothers and sisters in Christ, even learning from the occasional frictions. I learnt to accept authority.

Life change: marriage

Now in UESI for nearly three and a half years, I had learnt much. It was time to consider a respectable arranged marriage. Though it was not proper for a young woman to talk about marriage to her mother, who would make all the arrangements, I told my mother, 'If I am to marry, I want to marry a person who loves Jesus.' She could not understand. To her, any young man who went to church and was well educated would qualify for her daughter.

In the interval I met in my mother's friend's house a young man called Shadrach Peter. He found my address in Madras and wrote proposing marriage. I was affronted by his impertinence. He should propose through a senior person. It took me a year to cool down enough to speak to him, and then I was willing to talk over the possibility. He taught botany, zoology and chemistry in the Raichur Methodist High School, and his family lived in Raichur district. We had both given our lives to Jesus Christ and he meant everything to us. I was deeply touched by Shadrach's sincere faith and his zeal for God's work. To me this stood ahead of all other considerations. We told our parents we believed it was God's will for us to marry, and they were happy. They made all the other wedding preparations. We prayed that through our marriage and establishing a Christian home, Raichur would be blessed. It was the first wedding we had seen where the bride and groom on the stage at the reception shared their testimonies of how God worked in bringing this wedding to pass.

I think now that people like Shadrach and me are God's raw materials, shapeless to begin with, but moulded into shape by his hands. Two days into our honeymoon we were planning, budgeting, drawing up lists and writing notes for a camp for college students. Spiritually dry Raichur and neighbouring Gulbarga and Bellary would hold their first student Christian camp in thirteen days and we were given the key organizing role. It went well and about thirty students committed themselves to follow Christ. The speakers did a surprising thing. At the end of the five-day camp they called the students to one side and both of us to stand opposite. Pointing to the students they said, 'Shadrach and Gladys, look. Within fifteen days of your marriage God has given you this gift of so many children. Now look after them.'

This challenge caught fire in us. We responded, 'Yes, we'll do what God has given us to do.'

We lived in Raichur with my mother, keeping an open home for students. To let them savour the riches of the Bible, we held a weekly Bible study. Shadrach used to take three or four young men to a patch of big rocks nearby and, in the quiet, pray and give advice. For students living with their parents we made time to visit their homes to build rapport with their parents, so that the parents would feel able to trust us with their young people. We enjoyed life, and felt God was blessing us, especially when we could see students' lives changing as they trusted Jesus and brought other students to our home for personal counselling and Bible study. We used to go after the ones and twos and small groups, drag them towards the kingdom of God and then treat them like young plants that needed a lot of water, nutrients and sunshine to make them grow. That became a theme of mine – going after students for Jesus, never letting go, visiting people in their homes, inviting them yet again, having them stay in my house, mentoring, modelling.

A bitter pill

While we lived in Raichur our four children were born – Shobhna, Sharon, Sangster and Sweety. What times of joy we had and how they twined their lives through ours and our student friends' lives! But there was bitter-sweet as well. Our lovely Sharon, aged three months, became our first enormous heartache. After her first polio vaccination she contracted polio, undiagnosed for months.

Sharon's suffering shook us. We cried out, 'Please, God, help. Take this away.' She grew more ill. 'Where is God if he lets our baby suffer? Does God care?' We suffered too as we saw her limp and ill. Our days were full of pain. 'If God is in control, can't he thwart this disease?' A church member's words pierced our hearts: 'Perhaps you have committed some wrong and God may be punishing you.' Was something wrong with us? I blamed myself.

One day, disgusted with God, I sat in the last row of the church and questioned myself. 'How would it be if I threw God out of my life?' I suddenly felt as if I was enveloped in thick darkness. Everything went blurred. I saw myself make an enormous effort to leap out of this pit of unbelief and estrangement. I clung to God and said, 'I want you, Jesus, even in spite of the pain.' He comforted me till I felt as if I had been broken and he had put me together again. With all our troubled prayers, our weeping and uncertainty, we knew God was also giving us strength to keep going. We ran from one doctor to another with Sharon, first Raichur's, then big hospitals in

Vellore, Madras, Bombay. Our bodies were worn out, mentally and physically. Financial needs increased. In the distress godly friends came to our help. Sharon's muscle tone was permanently impaired. Next came the routine of teaching a tiny child to walk with callipers and crutches. Any small progress thrilled us, while it still hurt to see our little one unable to walk and run like other children. We knew we must be positive. She learnt along with the other children the verse, 'You are good, and what you do is good.' We and they came to know that God always gives his grace, even in the middle of suffering. Complaining was out.

Sharon is now an MA psychology student at Women's Christian College, Madras, majoring in the psychology of disability. Still walking with crutches and callipers, she wrote recently, 'To this day I don't wear lovely sandals and shoes. I obviously can't dance. I do walk a little slower than others. That doesn't put me off because I have learnt the secret of looking, not at what I can't do, but at what I can do. It is God who taught me to look at things the way he would want me to.' She rides off down the road on her two-wheeler adapted with two extra wheels on the back wheel for balance, enjoying the freedom of mobility, and even the chance to take her friends on the pillion seat. God has also taught her to be gracious and to receive help when she needs to.

In addition to Sharon's polio, we faced illness for our youngest child, Sweety, loved by all but, at the age of three, weak and debilitated. We eventually found she had a rare blood disorder that demanded a blood transfusion every month. For years we took her monthly on the overnight train trip for the transfusions in Bangalore. She also needed a daily injection of Desferal, given through a syringe driver which required the needle to be prodded into her skin and left eight hours through the night. I felt so badly that Sweety had to have this, but she learnt to call that painful instrument her friend, because it would be beside her all night.

Home-based ministry

When the children were small, Shadrach and I had to plan carefully to keep some sense of balance in our lives. Sharon and Sweety needed lots of extra attention, but we could not neglect Shobhna and Sangster. We also wanted to care for our parents. Shadrach was teaching science full-time at the local high school. Sometimes a long string of students or house guests came to our house for advice or training. How could we be fair to both their needs and our children's? Sometimes I wondered if I was giving our children enough time. Yet pioneering student work in Raichur required that we put in time to build up the students and graduates as the people of God so that the fragile new work would not falter. Sometimes we felt torn in all directions, and prayed the harder that God would help us do justice in all the spheres of life where we were needed.

Once my mother grumbled, 'Why do you have to constantly feed so many people in the home?' This was hard. One is not supposed to go against parents. I explained gently but very clearly that our priorities were different. We would carry on feeding lots of people. She gradually saw the value of our work and understood, and at the same time we were glad to keep doing our best for our parents.

But at times, although I agreed heart and soul with our direction, I wondered if we should set some limits to our generosity. Shadrach's monthly salary of Rupees 200 ($60), was low even in the 1970s, but if a student could not pay a round of fees, Shadrach paid. Fine, he believed in giving, but the fee might be Rupees 100. What would we live on?

I remember pestering him after he lent twenty rupees to a teacher. 'Ask him to repay,' I muttered, when we saw the man.

Shadrach murmured back, 'The Bible says to give and ask nothing in return.'

Under my breath I groaned, 'How can I live with such a man?'

Somehow we survived, and God provided for our needs and kept the house full of laughter and chatting.

I remember a day when students were mixing the flour to make a cake for the Christmas get-together, excited because their Hindu friends were coming to join them. They planned to present the story of Jesus. Some formed a circle on the veranda and prayed for the programme. Some practised a song in the living-room. Some had gone to a bakery to ask if the cake could go in their oven as we did not have an oven. I had no time to think how much money was in the EU account, but I heard two of the young men discussing, 'We have just enough to pay the speaker's travel.'

Another added, 'What shall we do about rent for the auditorium?'

Then they both vanished into the back yard to pray for the needs of the programme. By the time it came, the bills were paid. God was faithful.

On a day of pouring monsoon rain a young Hindu woman walked two kilometres to read the Bible with me. Though she wanted to know more about Jesus, she was so unattractively sodden that I considered, 'How can I sit with her and study when she's so wet?' Somehow I knew what to do. I gave her a towel to wipe herself, a saree to wear, a cup of hot sweet tea, and then the Bible study. While I did it, I whispered to God, 'Why do you bring such needs that I'm bound to give what I have?'

The answer came in my daily devotion, from 1 Peter 4:9: 'Offer hospitality ... without grumbling.'

'OK,' I responded. 'I need to learn that doing right is not enough. I need the right attitude as well.'

This Hindu woman's family faced large problems over disputed land. She decided to follow Jesus if he would fix the problems. They were righted that night, and that woman became a convinced Christian who stood for Christ through thick and thin.

By the time Shadrach had taught high school for thirteen years, his salary had increased, God's work was progressing in the dry Raichur district, I was training young women in the Christian life and Shadrach was giving his evenings for young men. We were stretched yet contented, but God wanted one more stretch. We felt he said, 'Are you willing to give up your secure job and step out in faith to serve me?'

We said, 'We will support anyone else who steps out in faith.'

Back came the thought, which we believed was from God: 'I don't need your money. I need you.'

The UESI needed a Kannada-speaking person to build up the work across Karnataka with its forty million people. We knew we had to weigh up this, but the question lingered on. 'Would God supply all our needs with four children?' We had committed ourselves to God. We had to step out. In August 1983 Shadrach became a staff member of UESI.

For him it meant touring all over the state, meeting students, graduate groups and pastors, running meetings, organizing camps. One pastor asked me, 'How can you let you husband go when you need him so much?' Indeed, for me it meant managing at home without his help with four young children, two of them with health needs, and continuing to go after students to drill them, egg them on to live the Christian life and teach others as well.

I thought how my motto had become 'Never give up'. Students were constantly in the home either for personal counselling or for group studies. Frequently in the middle of cooking I would say to the latest arrival, 'Krishna, come into the kitchen, we'll cook and talk.' Both tasks got done, we ate and prayed, and a student could go on his way refreshed by both the spiritual and the mundane.

Once I made a list of the kind of questions the girls asked. Here are some of them: 'How can you say Rama is not our God when people have worshipped him for years?' 'My friends offer me prasad, the food offered to idols. Is it OK to eat it to avoid bad manners?' 'My parents are forcing me to consider marrying a Hindu. What shall I do?' 'My sins are serious. I'm guilty of ... What can I do?' Counselling, personal evangelism, building individuals in the faith – all this was going on. The ones and twos were entering God's kingdom, potential leaders were learning the ropes.

'Where is the money for this three days' camp?' a young leader asked.

'We'll start by asking for God's help.'

Sometimes people heard about our efforts and donated rice, lentils, or money. The students kept the purse and knew they had to spend wisely, buy only two kilograms of vegetables rather than a generous four. We chose camp directors among the simple, hard workers of the previous year. Those who led Bible studies at a camp would later be able to lead on a college campus.

We could see the changed life goals. 'What next after college?' I heard one ask another. 'I'm praying about theological study.' Another said, 'I would like to do that too, but my parents are not very willing.' 'I want to get equipped to teach God's word but I can't afford the fees.' We used to encourage them, persuade their parents, and write to friends to find donations for their fees. We loved seeing them get their degrees and come back to Christian work in Karnataka.

Women staff were scarce. I encouraged some young women to set aside marriage for a few years to work for UESI. Sometimes I had them stay in my home for one or two years as a kind of apprenticeship, going over their needs informally at any time of the day. Our children got used to having extras with the family and the visitors enriched them, though now and again the needs clashed.

One day Shadrach landed at home with a guest and came to the kitchen saying, 'Serve some food, whatever is cooked.' I stood in the middle of the children who had just come in from school. One was crying, 'Mummy, tomorrow I have a maths exam. I need your help,'

I blurted out in a controlled whisper, 'Why did you bring him home for dinner without telling me?'

Shadrach apologized. 'Give him food first. I'll see what's left and have that.'

Times like that taught me that God is in control of our lives. He knows whom to bring into our homes. I needed to accept them peacefully.

Marriage matters

In India churches do not give counselling about marriage, young people are not allowed to make friends or discuss marriage, and parents do not talk about it; they just make the arrangements. Increasingly we gave advice on finding life partners. We acted as parents for some, helping them find suitable partners, and in other cases shared with parents on the suitability of a proposal for their son or daughter. We felt it important. We wanted these students to marry Christians and build Christian homes. Without advice, they might have had to marry non-Christians.

Once after church on a hot day we got home and heard a knock at the door. A Christian woman rushed in saying, 'Why are you brainwashing our children and teaching them to disobey their parents?'

Shadrach and I sat stunned till we slowly said, 'What happened?'

She continued shouting. 'My son wants to marry a girl who is not our choice and he says he has talked to you about it.' We kept listening. 'Why do you meddle in our family affairs? You keep your hands off or it will be serious.'

She left in a huff while we sat silent, children and guests too, numbed by the onslaught. Yes, he had shared with us some of his thoughts on marriage. Pained, we committed this to God. Ten years later this lady became a very good friend.

'Women submit. Women be silent. Women are second-class citizens. Women must cook, and meet their husband's and children's needs. Husbands are bosses and caretakers.' These were the family laws of Raichur for both Christians and Hindus. We decided to put on the first Family Seminar to give biblical teaching on marriage.

'But my husband will never change. This is my fate,' a woman moaned when we invited her.

One husband said, 'What is there to learn about a Christian home? We are Indian and we cannot imitate western ideas.'

Finally four or five couples, full of apprehension, met at the riverside near Raichur. We made husbands and wives sit together. Unheard of! They never sat together openly at home. We told husbands how to care for wives, how to give them dignity, how to care for children, how to resolve husband–wife conflicts and in-law disputes. We bought fresh river fish and cooked it under the trees. For lack of hotels and money, we slept as couples on a verandah under the starry sky. The highlight to me was persuading them to go for a swim together. They had never dreamt of such a thing. The women dipped in the water still wearing their sarees, of course, but they enjoyed play and relaxing with their husbands. What a transformation! We were beginners in marriage courses, but we were starting a move towards better communication in Christian homes.

The nest is shaken

In 1991 we moved to Bangalore to continue our work of discipling students. Shadrach continued travelling for UESI. Sweety, now thirteen, was still a sick girl and her condition became serious and life-threatening. On the advice of doctors we decided on a bone-marrow transplant at Christian Medical College Hospital at Vellore. Her sister Shobhna would be the donor.

One day during our family prayer time Sweety said, 'What will happen if I die in the operation?'

We froze painfully. What could we say? Within a minute she answered her own question. 'So what, I'll be the first one from our family to be with Jesus.'

She loved her friends. She used to meet with two classmates for prayer in her lunch break at school, and often spoke about Jesus to doctors and nurses during her transfusions.

For the transplant, Sweety had to stay in a sterile room with one family member allowed to visit her one hour each day. On Shobhna's visit one day, they laughed and talked and then read Psalm 121. To encourage her sister Shobhna said, 'Jesus is always with you, while you eat or drink or sleep.'

Sweety stopped Shobhna. 'You just read that he neither slumbers nor sleeps. He's awake watching over me.'

She practised the presence of God as she grew more frail with the complications that set in. Her life was ebbing away. How sadly we watched her!

With a Christian doctor I sang into her ears so that, with her eyes closed, the last words she would hear were about Jesus. For me as a mother it was like a lullaby for Sweety, gently passing her on to Jesus from my arms. Thus far he had given her to us as a trust and now I gave her back to him. It was 12 March 1994.

Sweety's funeral was a beautiful service attended by hundreds of young people and friends. Both Sharon and I spoke of the goodness of God in Sweety's life and how she had enriched our lives. After the funeral, how we missed her at home! Her shoes, her books, her room reminded us. I started questioning God's goodness and trustworthiness. Sweety had trusted God, trusted to her death. As I kept looking at this pain I felt God said, 'I am with you in your pain and grief.' I did not ask for the pain to go, but God was with me. Sometimes I wished it did not have to be me. In the middle of such thoughts a friend's letter arrived quoting 1 Corinthians 15:58, '... stand firm. Let nothing move you. Always give yourselves fully to the work of the Lord, because you know that your labour in the Lord is not in vain.' That solved my problem. I did not want to live, but if I lived, then let me abound in the work of the Lord. This verse gave me a purpose to live again.

As I write this, Shadrach is completing his Masters degree in theology, Shobhna is working as an assistant lecturer in a college of nursing, Sharon is in England briefly for a consultation on Christian response to disability, and Sangster is studying his pre-university course. I keep on with student work. I feel useful and fulfilled. Wherever I am invited I speak of Jesus and what he is teaching me through many experiences. God's dealings with us are for a purpose. I have much to thank God for. He brings wholesomeness into my person and deals so graciously with me. In spite of all the human frailties he doesn't give up. I follow after him.

Chapter 3

Rebecca Atallah

Vivienne introduces Rebecca

In the early 1980s I first met Rebecca Atallah (née Wilkinson) with her husband Ramez at IFES student conferences on the Mediterranean island of Cyprus. Later I was a guest in their home in Cairo on several occasions in connection with our pioneer student work in the Middle East. Once in the mid-1980s another colleague and I had an unexpectedly prolonged stay with the Atallahs when rioting erupted and a curfew was imposed, suddenly restricting citizens to their homes in Cairo. My plane for Bahrain did not even try to land in Cairo. Rebecca, who with her family lived in an apartment block in Heliopolis, called on several of her mostly Muslim neighbours to see if they had adequate basic supplies and to offer Ramez's help in collecting children from school. I realized the influence of her gracious neighbourliness on the community. The next time I met Rebecca was in 1988 at Schloss Mittersill, Austria, at an annual consultation for our small regional Middle East and North African team. We also met on my subsequent visits to

Egypt, and now most recently in the autumn of 1998, when Rebecca spent six days with me in Cyprus at my Paphos home, writing most of this chapter.

Like me, you will appreciate Rebecca as you follow her story in three cultures. She shared in revival among students in Montreal and among garbage collectors in Cairo.

Rebecca tells her story

It all began in Haiti

I was born in 1947 in Haiti, West Indies, of missionary parents, who served the Lord there for eighteen years. My parents lived most of the time in the backward, rural interior of what is still the poorest country in the western hemisphere. They learned French, spoken only by the educated, and Creole, the dialect of all Haitians. At that time Haiti was officially Catholic, but most of its people were Voodooists, whose religious cult involved witchcraft and communication by trance with ancestors and animistic gods. Very few churches existed in the interior, but God used my father to start thirteen. He travelled a great deal, so it was mostly up to Mom to raise their six children. She lovingly taught us to know Jesus, to read and write, and to handle the stresses of being the only non-Haitians in our town. She also coped with the dozens of people who came to the house each day with their varied requests for help.

Four daughters were born (I being the second), and the fifth child turned out to be their much-prayed-for boy. Then God in his wisdom gave them a blue-eyed girl whom they soon realized was mentally handicapped. She was also a severe epileptic, and now, at thirty-nine, is still one of the greatest enigmas to some of the best neurologists in North America. In spite of the best medications, two brain surgeries and very patient and loving care by my parents, she has continued to have multiple seizures, often daily. We have often asked 'why?' and have regularly asked God for healing, but have finally accepted that God's ways are past finding out (Rom. 11:33). Rosy has had a permanent effect on each of us siblings, helping us to have compassion on all kinds of suffering. We have all become involved in some way with the marginalized of society, and I feel that my work with the poor and refugees has partly come out of those early memories of living with and loving a precious little girl who had suffered incredibly all of her life, but usually with patience and joy.

I remember my childhood as being extremely happy. The only real pain, other than Rosy's, was being sent away to school and thus separated from my wonderful family. We were all home-schooled, but when I was ten I was sent to receive some formal education in the capital city, Port-au-Prince. I lived with missionary families, attending an American school where I was surrounded by many different nationalities and faiths. Undoubtedly this contributed much to my ability later on to live comfortably in a pluralistic setting. Through this experience I also started learning to love and trust God independently of my family. In fact, I remember vividly how my sense of homesickness would drive me each day to rise early and have my quiet times nearby in an old, abandoned fort.

When I was twelve, my parents and their mission, UFM International, decided that they should move to Port-au-Prince to help in the forming of a national Christian college. So, to my joy and delight, we were again reunited. Dad continued this work for the next six years, and at the same time was able to help in the beginning stages of IFES work in Haiti. The student movement established at the Université d'Haiti has often been weakened through the continual political and economic woes of the country, with its resultant brain-drain as thousands of the well-educated have fled to the West.

Adolescence in a new country

When I was fourteen, our family took leave in the USA, so I left my beloved Haiti. When my parents returned after a year, my older sister and I stayed for further education, and I lived with a wonderful Christian family in Detroit, Michigan. Though separation from both family and my birth-country was painful, it was a growing and stretching time for me. It was then, at sixteen, that I received my calling from God to be a missionary some day.

By my first year in university, my parents had decided to leave Haiti, as a strong national church had developed under Haitian leadership and my father, with his pioneering spirit, felt that perhaps there were other lands which needed him more. God guided them to Quebec, Canada, which in 1965 had very little French-speaking Protestant work or influence. This major move presented me with a quandary. I had always wanted to be a nurse, and had almost landed a scholarship at a well-known nursing school in Detroit. So what to do now? Having experienced four lonely years of separation from my family, I was not the rebellious teenager just dying to leave home. I accepted that God must be leading me elsewhere, since he was obviously leading them. I gave up my vocational dreams. Looking back, I realize what an important decision that was, for it totally changed the course of my future life.

Remarkable years in MCF

Instead of becoming a nurse, I entered McGill University in Montreal and double-majored in French and English literature. I wanted real fluency in French, having mostly learned Creole as a child. That first year was tough. The Canadian system was very different from the American, and McGill was very demanding academically. The winters in Canada practically killed us all. Haitians were an extremely friendly, open people with a rural mentality, while the Canadians were rather reserved. In addition, Quebec-French was almost a different language from Haitian-French.

Dad got involved with French-speaking students at the Université de Montreal and, along with a few others, started what would later burgeon into the now independent, IFES-related movement of the Groupes Bibliques Universitaires. Adjusting to two different western countries in a relatively short time was difficult for us children. My grades plummeted and my feet froze, as I had to hitchhike to class during several of Montreal's infamous bus strikes. I was surrounded by agnostic students living rather hedonistic lifestyles and was continually challenged by cynical professors. I had either to sink or learn to swim, and what better place to do the latter than in McGill's Inter-Varsity chapter? Through IV I learned to think biblically in a very unchristian intellectual environment, and to witness in a large, confusing campus which was actually hungry for truth.

Our group, McGill Christian Fellowship (MCF) was a motley crew, coming from French and English backgrounds, with many other cultures represented. Our denominations ranged from High Church Anglican to Pentecostal. But we had two things in common: we needed each other if we were to survive spiritually, and we dearly wanted to share the good news of Jesus with our hungry, hurting campus. Most of us were certainly neither experts in evangelism nor especially gifted intellectually. But God was at work at McGill, and he was willing to use anyone, even us, and so things began to happen. We had several Bible studies a week in both male and female residences, and prayer meetings at various times of the day, starting at 6:00am and ending late at night. We also had campus-wide outreach programmes at the beginning of each academic year. Our strategy was to invite a well-known speaker to spend several days with us, giving a series of talks on campus and also conducting debates in different faculties and residences. These meetings were usually well advertised with a banner right in the middle of the main campus and with such titles as 'Jesus Christ: God or Superstar?' We preceded these missions with door-to-door visiting in the residences, inviting students to come and later following them up with Bible studies for enquirers and new believers. So it became impossible to hide our identity as Christians. Anybody who attended McGill in the mid-1960s became aware that there were students on campus who thought everyone should and could know God.

Our group became, understandably enough, very cohesive and close. We became best friends, and many of us remain in touch with each other until this day, over thirty years later. Many have gone on to become missionaries and pastors, and the Anglican Church in Quebec was to be revolutionized in the 1970s and 1980s by the many former McGill Christian Fellowship students who went into the Anglican ministry. I was incredibly blessed by being a member of that group for those three years. Although it was tough going, it helped to make me strong, and much surer of my faith than I would have been had I, for example, just attended a Bible college.

Swept off my feet by an Egyptian

God gave me another great blessing through following my parents to Quebec. I had never met an Egyptian; in fact I hardly knew where Egypt appeared on the map. So when, in my first year at McGill, an Egyptian guy phoned to invite me to MCF, I was intrigued and flattered. But the wind was taken out of my sails when I discovered that he had done the same for two other new female students. Ramez always went out of his way for everyone, and he had a contagiously enthusiastic view of life and ministry. He did everything he could to advance the kingdom of God at McGill University. Understandably, he was twice elected the president of MCF. He was easy to fall in love with, being so concerned and loving to everyone, but he soon made it clear that he had no thoughts whatsoever of marriage to any of us, as he had been called by God to return to his own country.

Ramez had immigrated with his family to Canada in 1962, and had met the Lord in a personal way just a few months later, at the age of sixteen. Always a visionary with a burning desire to help his people, he had soon realized that a relationship with God through Jesus Christ was what they needed most. When he met this American girl, at a time when Egypt and the United States were on bad terms, he was not about to get personally involved with her. I, on the other hand, quickly recognized that he had the qualities I believed I wanted in a husband.

Well, we definitely fell in love. Ramez wouldn't admit it, for he had always said he would never tell a girl he loved her until he was ready to marry her. Much more in touch with my feelings than he was, I knew how I felt and was pretty sure he felt the same. But this crazy principle of his to not marry a westerner – what to do about that? The only solution, which I had well learned in other tough times, was to pray about it. Evidently the Lord agreed with me, for he started changing Ramez, even in the area of his 'principles'. He showed him that it was not the nationality that counted, but the heart. It was not the passport I carried, but rather the willingness to go where he would go, and make his people my people (Ruth 1:16). So, after graduation, we were married on 29 June 1968. All of MCF was there. Little did we know, when we tearfully left MCF, how soon God would bring Inter-Varsity, then IFES, back into our lives. And how long it would actually take us to get to Egypt.

The early years of marriage

Ramez had obtained his Master's degree in social work, so for our first year of marriage he worked as a child protection officer in Kingston, Ontario, while I learned to be a wife. During this time we were also associate staff members for Queen University's IV chapter. Then we moved for three years to the USA, to Gordon-Conwell Theological Seminary, in Boston, Massachusetts, to fulfil Ramez's dream of doing further biblical studies. Rather miraculously, I was able to get a job as a medical social worker, even though I had never had any social-work training. I spent three challenging years learning the profession. In the last twenty-five years, I have often seen how God used this training as preparation for my work with the poor.

We had assumed that we would move to the Middle East soon after Ramez received his Master of Divinity degree from Gordon-Conwell. But God had other plans. Ramez ended up instead accepting the position of Divisional Director for Inter-Varsity in the Province of Quebec. Thus we moved back 'home' to Montreal for eight of the most exciting and fulfilling years of our lives and ministries. Again, God had surprises in store.

Miracles in Montreal

For me, this period was special because it enabled me to concentrate on being a mother, and allowed me to raise our children near to both our families. Joel was born in 1973, and Leila in 1976. In their early years of bonding to their grandparents, I learned from both sets of parents how to mother. I became an ardent, stay-at-home-mom supporter, as a letter I wrote in 1979 to the *Montreal Gazette* revealed. In it, I protested against an article which had suggested that the biggest change our society needed in order to truly liberate our families was for more and better community day-care service facilities for children, countering that rather we needed more dedicated moms and dads who would be willing to sacrifice their personal ambitions for their children's sake.

During those years in Montreal, I became a Canadian citizen. I had come to love this vast, beautiful country with its million lakes, and also felt that travelling would be easier and safer using a Canadian passport.

As well as raising children, I was involved in various ways with the poor, mainly through working with Haitian refugees who attended my father's church and through being an associate staff member of World Vision of Canada. This latter contact was very fruitful, if not in the actual amount of money I raised for World Vision, at least in my own training in Christian international efforts to help the poor and needy throughout the world.

I also had a new encounter with the Holy Spirit. Becoming increasingly aware of the vast needs of the poor, I realized my inability to cope emotionally with all of this knowledge. This led me to cry out to God for him to fill me again with his presence and his power, and he did just that.

Being Director of Quebec Inter-Varsity at first meant that Ramez worked entirely in English. But in the 1970s God did an awesome thing in French Canada, and we started seeing dozens, then hundreds of French students converted. Quebec society had largely moved away from its strict Roman Catholic roots, and had become quite secularized, creating a spiritual vacuum with resulting moral confusion keenly felt by the younger generation. In our IV work, we found young people very open to the gospel and easily led to faith in Christ. No-one had anticipated this; in fact, Protestant missionaries and pastors working in Quebec for twenty years had previously seen very few conversions. The churches were not prepared for it, nor was Inter-Varsity. New French-speaking churches started springing up, to provide for this burgeoning group of new converts. At one stage in the 1970s it was estimated that a new French Protestant church was being planted every week.

Thus began the Groupes Bibliques Universitaires du Quebec,

as small groups of students banded together in many of the colleges and universities. Ramez found himself working more and more in French (he had been raised knowing Arabic, English and French). Much of my counselling with students was in French and it was the toughest counselling I had ever done. These kids had been marred by their years of living without God and without morals. Materially they had everything they needed, but emotionally they felt empty, far from their original French-Canadian roots in family and church. Many of them were involved in Quebec's struggle to win independence from Canada, but even that was proving elusive and unsatisfying. Out of this social vacuum came spiritual hunger, and God used it in beautiful ways to bring many to himself.

Leaving success for the unknown

After being in Quebec for eight years, we began to ask ourselves if our former 'calling' had actually been a mistake, and whether we should spend the rest of our days in the fulfilling ministries in which we were involved. But God never allowed us to forget the Middle East. I always had within me a sense of uneasiness, even restlessness, as I felt us getting more and more settled in Quebec. We had resisted buying an apartment or house, thinking we would not be staying that long. As our children became settled in schools, we started wondering if we should consider such a purchase. That brought everything to a head.

As has often happened since, taking off a specific period of time to fast, pray and seek God's leading helped us to understand his will clearly. God answered in a way we could never have anticipated. The year before, we had travelled to Egypt for a couple of weeks, the first visit for Ramez in seventeen years, to 'scout out the land', especially looking into two job and ministry opportunities. Although at the time we had felt more drawn to the second work, it was the IFES offer to Ramez of developing work in Egypt that continued to impress itself upon our hearts as being right for us.

Earlier, Ramez had approached our Swiss friends the Decrevels (whom we had met at Gordon-Conwell) to replace him in GBU, but they had refused. Ramez had had similar experiences in other areas of his responsibilities in IV. We had thus concluded that leaving Quebec IV was not the Lord's will, at least not yet. However, during that weekend, it was as though God said, 'Approach these people again.' He also showed us other steps to take to free us to leave IV, and gave us assurance that we were to move to Egypt. So we obeyed. Upon returning home, we phoned our parents and told them we would be moving in seven months. We then informed both the French and English branches of IV, and wrote again to the Decrevels in Switzerland. To our amazement, they agreed this time to come and head up GBU. Another faithful and long-time staff member of IV, Ken Bresnen, agreed to replace Ramez as Director for the English work in Quebec. (Historically, this linguistic division of responsibilities was very important, as it paved the way for GBU, which only ten years before had been almost non-existent, to become a completely independent member of IFES.) As we burned our bridges behind us, things continued to fall into place. Saying goodbye was the hardest part. On 24 August 1980, we left our beloved families, friends and country and moved to Cairo.

Egypt at last: cultural adjustments

We bantered good-naturedly for a few minutes, the old man and I. With his white, bushy beard and his beautifully lined face, set above a long, flowing gallabeyya, he looked more like a figure out of *Arabian Nights* than a lemon-seller in our suburb of Heliopolis. We each tried to convince the other of the right price for that bag of lemons, but I soon gave up, reflecting that he undoubtedly needed the money more than I did. As I handed him a pound, he very courteously gave it back to me, insisting that I keep it. I, of course, did the same, asking him to please accept it 'for my sake', and the transaction was finally completed. It had taken me almost five minutes to buy a bag of lemons.

While driving home, I reflected how this incident illustrates two of the things I love best about Egypt: its contradictions and its people. It is a land of extreme contrasts, and if one really stops to notice them, one can never be bored here. Frustrated, yes; annoyed, certainly; furious, often, but never bored. Side by side you see Mercedes and garbage carts, totally veiled women and ones who seem to leap out of a fashion show, and deeply courteous people who seem to forget all their politeness when behind the wheel of a car. You marvel at the seemingly timeless existence of the pyramids and on the way home admire a very modern skyscraper. You take weeks trying to get just one paper signed at a government office, then discover that your neighbour's third cousin on his mother's side just happens to be an official in the right office and can get it done for you in ten minutes. You despair at the inefficiency and dirt of some of Cairo's hospitals, but then, in an emergency, discover that some of the world's best doctors are here, and are willing to make house calls.

These were some of the reasons why I quickly fell in love with this country. The Egyptians, though so traditional and family-centred, welcomed us with friendliness and warmth, delighting in our differentness and asking questions, questions, and questions. They adored our children, and Leila had to get used to having her blond curls continually patted by strangers on the streets. Often, when walking down main streets in our middle-class suburb, I would feel transported back to my childhood in Haiti, with its car horns constantly blaring, its open-air markets, its carcasses hanging in bloody display in front of the butcher shops, and its friendly people inviting me in for a cup of tea. It was a totally different country, religion, race and political system from those I had been raised in, but still so, so similar. In short, I felt I was coming home.

What they don't tell you in newsletters

We rented a large, rather decrepit apartment on a main street in Heliopolis (a suburb of Cairo), where we remained for over nine years. My neighbours in our building of nine apartments became my new family. Their many children, some of whom were rather neglected by their overworked parents, rang our doorbell constantly. They were a source of continual comfort when I so desperately missed Rosy and my many nieces and nephews. For the first few months, Ramez and I mostly concentrated on surviving. Our place needed an enormous amount of repair and he – always handy with his hands – became a resident electrician, plumber and carpenter, even being asked at times to work on our neighbours' flats. In fact, when our four-year-old was asked at nursery school what her father did for a living, she replied in all sincerity, 'Oh, he fixes houses.' Not having a telephone was very trying, but it also helped us to get to know our neighbours on the street, some of whom had phones. Buying food was a continual challenge, as in those days there were no supermarkets, only small, local grocers with a very limited variety of goods. In fact, once I calculated that to get a week's groceries I had to shop in twelve different stores.

Back to school with my children

We started attending two churches, both within walking distance – one in Arabic and the other in English. The former was large, well organized and completely Egyptian, the latter small and floundering but with a breadth of nationalities, languages and denominations. To this day, we are members in both churches.

Learning Arabic was my biggest challenge. What a tough language it turned out to be! I immediately enrolled in a nearby language centre, and later also took private lessons with an excellent teacher of Egyptian Arabic, Laila Kamel. She ended up becoming one of my closest friends, and during that period also made a personal commitment to Jesus Christ. (She also accompanied me the first time I visited the Mokattam Garbage Village, where we are both still happily involved, seventeen years later.) With Laila's tutoring and my neighbours' friendships, I learned fast, finding that having a second language made it much easier to learn a third. In the Arabic church, our children felt out of place, so I attended Sunday school with them to help translate. As soon as I could memorize some Bible stories in Arabic, I started teaching there. They soon passed me up as they made Egyptian playmates, and now are far more fluent than I can ever hope to be.

We enrolled Joel and Leila in a local, British-system, Egyptian-administered school. Their schooling proved to be God's greatest way of teaching us to trust. Partly due to internal problems, and partly because of the owner's constant conflicts with the education authorities, the school regularly almost shut down. Time and again, we prayed that it would stay open and that the Lord would provide good form-teachers for the children, and again and again he miraculously answered.

An untraditional student strategy

Helping to bring to birth an Egyptian IFES-related movement proved to be very different from any student work we had ever done before. The political structure of the country did not allow any religious groups, Christian or Muslim, to meet on educational campuses. Most of the Coptic and Evangelical churches in Cairo have regular youth meetings for different age groups on a weekly basis. Ramez had to learn different approaches, relevant to the different political and church scene of the country. He found that the model best suited to Egypt was that of Norway and other Scandinavian countries, where the IFES-related ministry is part of the Lutheran Church's youth ministry. Colin Chapman, a former IFES Regional Secretary for the Middle East, had already established this approach in the late 1970s. The 1980s, then, were a time to develop the ministry in a way that suited the particular context. Our task was to assist the Evangelical churches in Egypt in their ministry to students. So we linked up with three different student movements (two university and one high-school) and attempted to help each develop in the best way possible. Ramez's greatest involvement turned out to be with the National High School Committee of the Evangelical Church. Those were exciting days and some of the best youth leaders in Egypt were involved in ministry to high-schoolers through church groups in every part of the country.

Alongside this ministry within the Evangelical Church, God opened up in a remarkable way an inductive Bible study ministry in the Youth Bishopric of the Coptic Orthodox Church. This resulted in the establishment of the St Timothy Centre for inductive Bible study, which still today helps train Coptic Orthodox students in leading Bible studies.

During those nine years with IFES in Egypt and the Middle East, I was too busy learning Arabic, raising children and helping our family just to survive to assist very much in the student work. Of course, I did a lot of entertaining. In Egypt, when someone comes to the door it is polite to invite him or her in, and offer a cup of tea or a cold drink. The number of glasses and cups I washed in a single day sometimes staggered me. Being hostess to students, IFES staff and various Christian leaders associated with the work of the region kept me involved, even though not as completely as I would have liked. Opportunities also arose to help at student conferences for the Arab world held in Cyprus (the only country in the region safely accessible to all).

Unable to leave Egypt

During the 1980s, Ramez became widely known as the 'Bible study' man. This eventually led to his being invited to become General Secretary of the Bible Society of Egypt. This was a difficult decision to make, as he was at that time a candidate for becoming General Secretary of the IFES, and he and I had already gone to England for an interview. Student work seemed his forte. He spoke three languages, had led student movements in three cultures, and felt that it was time to 'reach for the world'. When he frankly asked Joel, Leila and me what we felt about moving to England, we all said we would go along with him if he took the job, but that we would really much prefer staying in Egypt, which had become our home, all three of us now even holding Egyptian as well as Canadian passports.

After much prayer and soul-searching, in August 1989 Ramez withdrew his name from the IFES candidacy. We hated to think of leaving this organization which had meant so much to us and where we had seen God's power so beautifully displayed. Vocationally, it was also taking a risk, for the Bible Society offer had not yet been formalized and we had no assurance that Ramez would be the final choice. But we all were sure it was the right decision. God had again called us to Egypt.

A garbage boy changes my life

In 1982, God led me into a totally unexpected area, one I didn't even know existed when still living in Canada. It all began on our first morning in Egypt, when a young, dirty teenager with a large basket slung over his shoulder knocked on our door. He wore clothes I wouldn't have used as rags. When Ramez asked what he wanted, he explained that he would be coming every day to collect our garbage, which he would then take home, the foodstuff to feed to the family's animals and all the rest to recycle. This boy, Salah, was our introduction to the garbage people of Cairo, and from the first I felt my heart strangely attracted to him and his situation.

Over the next two years, while studying Arabic, I learned a lot about the garbage people through Salah. He explained that he and his dad rose before sunrise each day to come by donkey cart from their ghetto to our area, where he collected the trash from every apartment. Returning home, they would turn it over to the women of the family for sorting with their bare hands, into piles of plastic, cardboard and glass for recycling. I couldn't imagine the filth and unsanitary conditions they must be living in, but the stench of Salah's clothes told it all.

Because of the nature of their work, as well as the fact that most garbage people were Christian, at least in name, they tended to be despised by the rest of Egyptian society. They were considered the lowest class in this very class-conscious land. As I asked around, I realized that very few people had ever been inside one of the seven garbage villages in Cairo. Thus they were also very cut off from ministry and services of any kind. I prayed a lot for these people and became convinced that God wanted me to have some sort of ministry with them.

Experiencing God in the Mokattam

When I visited the Mokattam Garbage Village, hidden away in the hills right in the centre of Cairo, I met Father Simon, a Coptic Orthodox priest, who had been ministering in that village for eight years. He told me that several years before, while still a layman, he had led his garbage boy to Christ. Coaxed by the boy to come and share the gospel with them, Father Simon, at that time named Farahat, had finally gone to their village and found a group of about 17,000 people in what was a living hell. They had no running water or electricity, no schools, churches, stores, clinics, or other services. They did, however, have coffee houses where they could buy alcohol, thus further contributing to a despair which caused the men to abuse their families and never to consider trying to better their situations.

These people knew nothing about the love of God for them but seemed to be spiritually hungry. They responded very well when Farahat and his friends on subsequent visits talked about Jesus and his offer of salvation. Soon there was a rapidly growing group of believers, and many miracles, both physical and spiritual, were reported in those early days. Things changed rapidly as these people were filled with the love and power of the Holy Spirit and motivated to do something to help themselves and their families. Instead of simply drinking away their meagre earnings, they began saving to build small homes, replacing their cardboard and tin shelters with stone and brick buildings. For the first time in their lives, they realized that, although they worked with garbage and lived with garbage, they themselves were not garbage.

The garbage people soon started wanting a church building, so after God showed Farahat in a vision that he was to devote the rest of his life in service to them, they asked the Coptic Orthodox Church to ordain him as their pastor and to help them to build a church. He became known as Father Simon. Under his enthusiastic, sometimes rough, and very simple leadership, the church grew very quickly. When I arrived in 1982, there was already a well-organized church with a small school meeting on its roof.

When my friend Laila and I saw that school, we realized that this was an area in which we could help, as it needed everything from pencils to classrooms. So began my love affair with the Zabbaleen (Arabic for garbage collectors), one which is still going on almost eighteen years later. I have been involved over the years with primary health visitation and with counselling, and am also mostly responsible for the Christian Education department of the school and for taking the children on field trips and summer camps which expose them to life outside their garbage ghetto. Laila helped to establish the 'Association for the Protection of the Environment', a factory where the poorest women and teenage girls learn skills of patchwork, rug weaving and recycling paper.

Father Simon and his wife, Soad, admitted to me that it had been very costly for them to come and live with their two small children in this ghetto of rubbish, pigs and violence. Although they have a small apartment in Cairo from which they were able to send their children to school, they spend every summer exclusively in the village, exposing themselves to many dangerous diseases including rabies and tetanus. Both children, however, have grown up loving the Lord and the garbage people, and are now involved, with their spouses and children, in service to the church and the hospital that has since been built there.

Father Simon's dream was to see the garbage collectors of Cairo one day serving the entire Egyptian church, thus fulfilling God's promise in 1 Corinthians 1:27 to use the weak and poor of the world to confound the strong and the rich. The discovery of a number of large natural caves just above the village has led to the fulfilment of that vision. One cave has been made into a church-amphitheatre with room for well over 10,000 people where weekly meetings are held, gathering Christians from all over Cairo. People are attracted both to the opportunity (unusual in the Middle East) to worship in a large group and to the hauntingly beautiful, peaceful setting of the cave churches.

This church of the poor now has the largest congregation in the Middle East, with garbage collectors and professionals, poor and rich, worshipping side by side, singing God's praises.

My involvement over several years in some of the poorest and filthiest homes in the village has enabled me to meet scores of women personally. I am constantly amazed by their contentment, despite their sometimes appalling living conditions. I think of Samia, married at fourteen and mother of nine, only four of whom are still living. She is still having kids, as her husband and mother-in-law want more help with the collecting and sorting of garbage. Since her oldest son lives with his family in Samia's small home, she is both mother and grandmother to tiny children, and works constantly both caring for them and sorting garbage. A vibrant and growing Christian, she has told me how God has helped her through the tough, heart-breaking times in her life. For her, knowing Jesus and counting on him and his peace makes everything seem different, allowing her to put into perspective her very hard circumstances.

Recently I have had the joy of being involved at the Mokattam Village with some of the disabled, handicapped and chronically ill people. Partly because of the common practice of intermarriage between cousins, there are many such people, including a large group of deaf. This ministry was begun, and is largely conducted and financed by, some of the young people of the village church. Of their own initiative, they collect most of the handicapped and disabled of the village (usually on foot) and take them to the church every week for services, recreation and fellowship. I have been involved mostly through helping to raise funds for special needs which the young people cannot afford out of their own tithes, such as extended hospitalizations, and running summer camps for the handicapped and disabled. Our children, Joel and Leila, are also involved with both the weekly programmes and the camps. They love it, and Joel has stated that one of the happiest periods of each year is the time he spends in the summers helping these people have a beautiful week at camp.

I love the garbage people intensely and consider some of them among my best friends. However, I have often been tempted to quit, sometimes in total despair in view of their seemingly hopeless situations, sometimes in exasperation with their very hierarchical, male-dominated structures. As an independent, Canadian woman with a Baptist upbringing, I have often found it difficult to worship and work in an Orthodox setting. At such times, I remind myself that God led me to go there and that I must not even dream of leaving unless he also leads me out. At other times, I simply look deep down in my soul and admit that I desperately need the garbage people. A big part of my identity and reason for living has become loving and working with them. They have also become my second family, helping to fill the void that separation from my own relatives had created.

God gives more than I can dare ask

I had always prayed, when in Egypt, that God would give me the privilege of being with my mother when she died, not only for my sake but also for hers. But I never really dared to believe it would happen, as we travelled to North America only every three to four years.

In early December 1996 Mom was unexpectedly diagnosed as having inoperable terminal cancer. Providentially, I was scheduled to speak a few weeks later at Urbana (the large, triennial IVCF missionary convention). The convention was three hours' drive from my parents' home in Indiana. Ramez's fare had also been paid by Urbana, and Leila was ending a six-month trip which brought her to her grandparents the day Mom's diagnosis was known. She was able to nurse Mom for the two weeks before I arrived. Our entire family of thirty people, except for Joel and his cousin Jeanna, was there for that last, memorable Christmas with Mom. She was alert, in tolerable pain and touchingly happy to have us all with her.

When eight of us travelled to Urbana on 26 December Mom had been given a few months to live. After the closing communion service, however, we learned that she immediately went downhill after we left. It was as though she had had all that she wanted, and was now ready to go. Mom was in a coma when we arrived home the morning of 1 January, and died that night, surrounded by most of her family, including three from Egypt. We sang hymns together. The moment we finished the last verse of 'It is well with my soul', she went to be with the Lord she had loved so much.

Blessed by the Sudanese

My life in Cairo also includes ministry among other groups of the poor and needy. Sudanese refugees have flooded into Egypt in the last few years as the war in Sudan has become more intense and cruel and as famine has afflicted the south. Many have very sad stories to tell of ethnic cleansing by the right-wing Muslim government in the north, of slave trade to other countries, and of systematic destroying of the homes of the southern Sudanese living in Khartoum. Side by side with these horror stories, we hear of wonderful revival going on in the churches, as God time and again visits his people in miraculous and life-changing ways. I am told that all churches in Sudan are filled to capacity, and that there is as a result a great lack of pastors, teachers and Christian literature. This revival is characterized by joy, a strange thing in the midst of such loss and deprivation.

Never have I met a people so genuinely generous and peaceful as the southern Sudanese. The past eight to ten years of service to them here in Cairo have taught our family many wonderful lessons about life, including the deep resources that God has placed within us all, which surface during crises and allow us to accept even pain and loss with joy.

I need the poor

If I have accomplished anything of real value in my ministry among the poor and needy, it has been through becoming a friend to some of them and their families. It is not in the new programmes I have started, or the money I have helped to raise. These, of course, are very helpful for those in need, but they are not the most important. These things will not last to eternity, except as they have helped to change the attitudes and characters of the people involved, including me. People last; programmes do not. In befriending some of the poor, I have made some eternal investments. I have been changed, and so have some of them. We have grown as persons, as children of the one Father, as we have grown as friends.

Chapter 4

Chun Chae Ok

Vivienne introduces Chae Ok

I first met Chae Ok in Pakistan when she came to join the staff of the United Bible Training Centre in Gujranwala in September 1969. Part of the activities of the Centre consisted of short courses for teachers, nurses, pastors' wives, college students, and school graduates. A considerable number of these short-course students appeared to be nominal rather than committed Christians. We prayed that they would come to personal faith in Christ before the end of their course. When Chae Ok arrived among us, she asked us why we did not pray for this to happen at the beginning so that the rest of the course could be building on a new foundation and establishing them in the faith. We prayed this way and God answered, so it became our practice.

Chae Ok and I also spent some time together in the UK at a retreat centre in Sussex for a period of reflection, rest and quiet. On two occasions I was her guest in Korea. On my last visit she and two of her friends took me to a church close to the United

Nations line dividing North and South Korea. Buddhists go there to face the North and pray for their ancestors buried in the North. Christians go to face the North to pray for the reunification of the country. We subsequently met briefly in Cyprus. We keep in touch through email, especially on matters relating to Islam.

Chae Ok tells her story

Birth, childhood and family background

Born in Korea in 1938, the youngest of a Buddhist family, I had three brothers and three sisters. My father was Principal of the Kong-Keun Primary School in Kang Won Province (now in South Korea). When I was five he moved to Kang Reng, a most beautiful east-coast city surrounded by the Sulak Mountains and the sea. My mother died when I was nine and my father three years later in 1950. They were both Buddhists.

My birthplace, Kong-Keun, is near Choon-Chun city, a lovely lake town. My brothers and sisters received schooling in Choon-Chun as Kong-Keun had only a primary school in those days. Kong-Keun is three hours' drive from Seoul. Some time ago I drove there to reflect on my early life. The public primary school is still there on a hillside near a small river. As a child I thought it was a very big and deep river, but this time, I saw it was only a small and shallow stream. I saw the spot where my father's house was located and where a new house has been built. The primary-school principal who lives there now was very gracious in welcoming me and we had a good chat over tea. To my surprise, he knew much about my family. He showed me around and I was very glad to see that the school, its garden and playground, are in very good condition. Classrooms were clean and the walls of corridors were decorated with attractive exhibits by pupils. I thought of my father, who started his teaching career there after his education in Seoul in Kyung-sung High School which is now the Seoul National University. In the garden in front of the house and near the gateway of the campus, there is a monument in memory of him. He was the Principal of the Kong-Keun primary school from 1932 until 1944. I spent the first six years of my life there until 1944 but I did not enter the primary school – it was my playground!

As to some of my siblings: Chae Hak, my second brother, died during the Korean war leaving his young wife with two boys and one daughter. My sister-in-law, a primary-school teacher, raised them well. My third brother, Chae Ho, died in 1994. His eldest son, Yoon-Kap, is close to me and used to come to worship with me in the University Chapel. He is an army officer, high up because of his computer-science expertise. His wife, a graduate of Ewha and now a professor in a theological seminary in Seoul, is also close to me. My seventy-eight-year-old eldest brother, Chae Chan, is well and lives in Seoul. He has ten grandchildren.

I meant to tell you about my early life with my parents. My father was a kind, capable teacher and administrator as well as a good father. He spent much time with me after his school before supper time. We walked in the school garden and I bicycled while he walked around. He taught me calligraphy. He combed my hair in the mornings and trimmed my pencils before my class. He often used to take us on picnics near the riverside, cooking fish from the river. We enjoyed rice and hot fish soup. He used to take us to the beach, an hour's bus ride away. My brothers went swimming in the sea but I walked on the sand with my father. He read Confucian classics. I remember he had a low book cupboard in his room with classical texts, such as 'the four books' of Confucius. He did not go to church but he had a younger sister who was a trained evangelist of the Methodist Church, and whose husband was a Methodist minister. So he must have heard the gospel and possibly read the Bible. However, I do not remember any Bible in my father's house in my early days. In the summer of 1944 he moved to Kang Reng City, the largest city in Kang-won province on the east coast, becoming Principal of Oak-Chon primary school for three years. Then in 1947 he left to become the Principal of the Kang-Reng public primary school, which had 2,000 pupils at that time, as I remember from a verse in the school song. My father died of a stomach disease during the first year of the Korean war. Neither he nor any of the family were Christians.

In 1946 when I was nine, my mother, who was very active in arranging for the wedding of my second brother, Chae Hak, died suddenly one morning of a heart-attack when the wedding guests were still in the house. I remember that all the guests were so shocked. According to old-fashioned culture, they thought the bride had brought this ill fortune to my family. My mother was a business woman who took care of the farm land and forest which our grandfather had left in In-Je town. My father did not get engaged in such business and it was mother who collected the harvests. My mother was a hospitable housewife who liked to have many guests for meals. She was a thoughtful hostess. However, I do not remember much conversation with her. She was a good mother. I have only a few memories of her. When my sisters got together they told me that I am very much like my mother in my manner of walking and moving about, and in doing things. I have my father's album (no separate individual photos but general photos in the printed album prepared by the school) but no picture of my mother.

Our father treated all of us equally. There was no son-favouritism in our family. I received much love from my parents and brothers and sisters as I was so much younger than they. My mother was forty-two when I was born.

Early education

Until the Korean war, which broke out on 25 June 1950, I had a happy childhood attending the school where my father was Principal. After the Korean war and the death of my parents, things were different. My second sister and my brothers gave me schooling. My third sister and I stayed together from the high-school period as she was at the Ewha Womans University and I was in the Sook Myung Girls High School – named by the last queen, Min. It was one of the best girls' high schools at that time. However, it was not a Christian school. All my brothers and my other sisters were busy raising their families, but they gave me special support.

I was brought up in good health in every way – mentally and physically, with brothers and sisters, under quiet and firm parents who were not Christians. I received no gospel and had no chance to read the Scriptures until I ended my high-schooling at the age of nineteen. In my middle- and high-school times (during the war and after), I missed my parents and there was no faith that held me. During the Korean war for three years (my middle-school time) there was no good education because there were no teachers. We studied in an old, big Catholic church building because there were no school buildings. I suppose all the good buildings were destroyed by bombs. Principles such as sharing whatever we have, speaking the truth and learning diligently kept me going during my teens. I do not remember any Christian approaching me and urging me to trust Christ, except a friend of mine in the middle school who took me one day to a Christmas church meeting.

University education and conversion from Buddhism to Christ

I entered the College of Liberal Arts of Ewha Womans University in 1956. I was converted to Christianity in the second semester of the first year through reading the Bible and attending the compulsory chapel services. I read modern languages, English, French, and German, in the undergraduate programme while taking many other open courses.

The first Christian in my father's family

Nine of my family became Christians, but I was the first in the family to become a Christian. I remember attending a Sunday-school class when I was in primary school. But it did not make any permanent effect on me. Then, in the middle-school time, once again I went to a Christian youth class with my close classmate, Lee Sunsook, but soon stopped going. During high-schooling I do not recall going to church meetings. It all happened in the Ewha Womans University. There I decided to follow Jesus and study the Bible. I met Helen Kim, the first Korean woman PhD, and the President of Ewha. The chapel services and the course, 'Studies of Christianity', gripped me in the first year, and during the following four years in the university I attended church regularly after having received baptism in October 1956.

Missionary call

In the final year, through a chapel address given by Dr Helen Kim, I was called by God to missionary service in Pakistan as a Christian teacher. I volunteered to commit myself to go out to this unknown area and people in the province of Sindh. In the university I was influenced by Helen Kim, especially through her Wednesday special lectures given as an optional course called 'Women and Career'. She taught Ewha women to have a career besides raising families because they were the cream of Korean women, having had the privilege of receiving such quality higher education. Privilege means responsibility, she said. We must give, and by giving we receive. In those days, not many women in Korea had jobs in society. She challenged us to serve in society and in the world. Then she challenged us to know that it is God who calls us to work. She said the most important thing is to choose the first job, the first place and the first people to serve. We should choose work as our life-long task, not as a mere job to earn money. We are to have assurance that God calls us to do a particular job for his purpose. She taught dedication, commitment and loyalty. I owe much of my current values to her. She was a woman of fashion in her own revolutionary way. She wore modernized Korean costume all her life and had a very short-cut hairstyle. I learned the concept of beauty from her. She was single but she had a large family of students and teachers connected with Ewha. She had many guests all the time.

Helen Kim was a very loyal supporter of my missionary life and work until she was called to heaven. She wrote personal letters and showed much love in practical ways. After my commitment to serve in Pakistan, I had entered the Ewha Graduate School in 1960 in order to study theology as a preparation for going abroad. I followed Helen Kim in her itinerant preaching within the city and the country while I was a student in the Department of Christian Studies. My eyes were opened to the poor in the city and in the country. I had a longing to identify myself with them through serving them. My university friends of both sexes were very surprised at my changed attitude to life and values. Partying and mixed social gatherings for pleasure lost their attraction.

My attitude to marriage and family

I dedicated myself to be a missionary at the age of twenty-one in my final year as an undergraduate. Then I worked in the graduate school academically and also in voluntary services within Ewha University Church and in various rural areas.

When I attended my missionary dedication service, a great service led by Bishop Ryu, the first Korean Methodist bishop, I resolved that I would die for Christ and serve him only all my life. He was all to me. I had no space or time for thinking about marriage. Until I was thirty-six years old, I steadily held that attitude about marriage and family. Although there were a few beginnings of friendships, such friendships did not lead me to consider or commit to marriage. After my thirty-sixth birthday, although I was more open towards marriage, I did not think I could just marry just for the sake of it, especially as in Korea there is the custom of arranged marriages. I spent seventeen years abroad both for missionary work and theological studies and I am personally not open-minded about inter-cultural marriage. For fourteen years out of seventeen I was mostly surrounded by Pakistanis and English-speaking people. So that may be another reason for not being open for marriage. I do not regret it. It may be that this is due to my philosophy that there is no regret for anything past as I believe in the providence of God and the guidance of the loving Lord. What is important in life as a single woman is that I live a creative and loving life serving others. I do not say that it is the will of the Lord that I am single; rather I am saying that in my single state I am enriched by what I do and by what I am in the Lord. Whether single or married, what is important is to live an authentic life.

1960–74

As the first woman missionary supported by Ewha Womans University Mission and the Methodist Church in Korea I served in Pakistan from 1961 until 1974. I was engaged in student ministry with the Pakistan Fellowship of Evangelical Students (the PFES affiliated with IFES in 1975), and the Karachi Institute of Theology which later became St Thomas'

Theological College. I was Literature Secretary for the PFES. I became a member of the Cathedral Council, Karachi, Church of Pakistan, for two years. I also joined the staff of the United Bible Training Centre in Gujranwala, Punjab, for six months in 1969 to 1970. During my home leave in 1970 to 1971 I was a visiting lecturer at Ehwa Womans University.

My time in Pakistan influenced my thinking and attitude to life. The vast gap between the poor and the rich was a shock. When I met rich women, young and old, I wondered what they lived for in such a closed environment. It seemed their silk, gold, lamb curry meals, many children, and such visible comforts were everything to them. They did not seem to ask about the meaning of life and the purpose of being human. When I met poor women who had nothing but meagre meals, bare feet, undernourished children and illiteracy, I ached in my heart and wondered whether I could do anything meaningful for them. Life in Pakistan caused me to think about life and death. My fundamental and continuous question at that time was what it means to be liberated in and through Christ Jesus. It seemed to me that it is almost a crime to have a luxurious lifestyle when there were so many poor and hungry people. I thought that it was imperative to choose to live a simple life close to the poverty level in order to identify with the suffering poor.

Theologically and pastorally, I was influenced by the Reverend Geoffrey Bingham and Bishop Chandu Ray in the early 1960s. Later, during the period from 1965 to 1969, I was deeply moved to read and listen to the Reverend Dr John Stott. London Bible College lectures nourished me richly after the dry desert experience in Sindh, Pakistan. Dr Donald Guthrie and Dr Geoffrey Grogan and other London Bible College lecturers helped me greatly to think biblically and theologically. I drank deeply from the wells of good libraries on theology and from theologians of the West. At the same time I had a great longing for meditation and prayers. In fact, I think that I had my first authentic time of being a Christian in the desert. The desert gave springs of water in which to be washed and refreshed from time to time. My first five years in Sindh were an inexplicably rich experience of God the creator and the redeemer. I began to follow the way of the cross of Jesus in a real sense, not just intellectually and comfortably. Later, I received much help from Dr Donald McGavran and Dr Arthur Glasser at Fuller Theological Seminary in Pasadena, California, USA. They helped me to understand what mission is all about. I owe them a great deal for what I have taught since the late 1970s. At Fuller I learned about the history of the World Council of Churches and the Ecumenical movement as well as the evangelical movement fostered by the Lausanne Committee for World Evangelization and the World Evangelical Fellowship. I became aware of missiological issues and tried to understand how they might apply in my particular context. I was grateful to be able to record my fourteen years of missionary life in a book. My first year at Fuller was like finding diamonds by mining. I relished digging into the wealth of materials on missions. I wished I had had a longer time there. I was in too much of a hurry to acquire the degree. Whenever I think of Fuller, I have some regret at not prolonging my study and intellectual pursuits. I needed more academic struggle and interaction with others.

1977–99 in the context of Korea and the world

I was fortunate to be received on to the faculty of the Department of Christian Studies at Ewha immediately on arrival from Fuller in 1977. Dr Okgil Kim became the President of Ewha Womans University after Dr Helen Kim died. She had the same kind of concern and prayer for me as Dr Helen. In spite of her welcome and my homecoming to Ewha, I found it difficult to adjust to the life of teaching in the department. I had lived too much in a different world and culture. The source of my security and joy seemed to be different from that of my colleagues. I felt a stranger among familiar people, both family and friends. It was indeed the mercy of God which brought me through. I went through extreme pain and suffering in the first few years and sometimes thought that I could not endure more. The Lord's words in the Scriptures enabled me to hold on to God and cry to him. On the surface, I had security as an independent woman with a good career. I was often called upon to speak on missiological issues at different meetings and conferences locally and sometimes internationally. I travelled widely during vacations to attend conferences related to the WCC as well as the LCWE and WEF. Travelling abroad was a break and my friends commented that I always looked better after strenuous air trips. Right in my own environment, I found it difficult to be single. There was no unmarried woman in my department to identify with me, nor among my old classmates who became professors at Ewha. I found that living in an apartment was like a prison sometimes. I appreciated singing God's praises and reading the Scriptures together with others and yet I had to accept that there was no-one to share in the practical affairs of life despite the many occasions to minister to students and church people about mission and from the Scriptures. I knew acutely that a human being is a social being needing to interact with others. For this I experienced ample opportunities during the day on campus, but coming home was a threat of aloneness which I needed to overcome positively.

Miraculous healing

Liberation in my spirit, mind and body came in 1994 through being miraculously cured of a stone in my neck. I became more aware of the Lord's help and strength in my trouble. I had an appointment for an operation involving an incision of five centimetres on my neck to remove the stone. This proved unnecessary as the stone pushed itself out through my gums during my graduate seminar class. The students witnessed my taking the stone out from my mouth with my fingers without any touch of blood. It was a physical cure but somehow it meant more than that. I had a strong conviction of the Lord's presence. He took away fear. I think that I went through a valley of death and now I live in a new way. In all circumstances I became aware of God's love for me and for others.

I received awards from Ewha on the tenth and twentieth years of full-time teaching, as did other faculty members. For me it was the mercy of God. Then Fuller Theological Seminary School of World Mission gave me the 1991 Alumna of the Year award. It reads, 'In recognition of her outstanding contributions to the global missiological community as a field missionary, a scholar, and teacher, an international missions stateswoman and a devoted servant of her Lord, Jesus Christ.' This was also the mercy of the Lord.

Vivienne continues Chae Ok's story

Chae Ok was busy opening new courses in missiology, serving on committees and acting as a consultant. She initiated a course on the Theology of Mission in the Department of Christian Studies at Ewha. After that she started eight other new courses in missiology for graduate studies. Now there are several seminaries with missiologists catering for missiology. She became the President of the Missiologists Society in Korea from 1994 to 1996. For the first ten years of its existence she served on the Korea Overseas Missionary Fellowship Home Council. Currently she is a consultant to Interserve Korea and also a member of the Korean Council of the Society for International Ministries (SIM) and the Korea Inter-Varsity Christian

Fellowship Central Council. She has been an Executive Committee member of the International Fellowship of Evangelical Students (IFES) since 1995, and the President of the International Association of Mission Studies (IAMS) since its Eleventh Assembly in Buenos Aires, Argentina, in April 1996. She was the first Executive Secretary of the Missions Commission of the WEF from 1978 to 1981. She introduced the Reverend Dr Lee Tae Woong to replace her and now he is the Chairman of the WEF. She served two terms on the Central Committee of LCWE from 1978 and helped to start the Korean LCWE in the early 1980s.

Chae Ok resumes her story

In 1986 I wrote the story of my time in Pakistan, at the request of the editor of *Light and Salt* monthly magazine. In 1991 it was published in book form by Durano Publisher under the title *Pakistan – My Beloved*. It was a popular, not a laboured, work. It had five reprints and received very encouraging remarks from missionaries and missionary candidates as well as church people. The book covered all my years in Pakistan and contained sixteen stories including ones on desert women, an invitation to an engagement ceremony, the joy of learning Urdu, Pakistani church women, true neighbours, Muslim men, churches in Pakistan, revival movement in the Punjab, fruit during my sabbatical year, Muslim cultures, hospitality as mission, missionaries in Islamic cultures and a vision for unity in Christ. I wanted to convey my early experiences as realistically as I could and tried to recapture how I thought, saw, acted and reacted in those days. It is not a manual for missionary teaching but rather an account of how the first woman Korean worker for Christ in Pakistan survived. Some mission agencies use it as a required text for their training programmes. In 1986, I was in deep waters and writing those stories was salvation to me. After each period of writing (normally four or five hours in the early morning before I started off to campus for my regular class lecturing), I felt somehow relieved and liberated. I thank the Lord immensely for pulling me out from a dungeon through giving this task of writing. It was a time of reflection on myself and mission. After going through a long tunnel I wrote it by dim (symbolically) and flickering candle light, not being sure when it would be blown out, but I came out into a bright sunny open space in which to stretch myself and move normally.

They say that my writing has a quiet tone and rhythm and offers something to ponder on. If there is anything in my writing, it is my suffering and pain which the Lord used for his glory. I am thankful that I have a gift to give my students and missionaries. These days I have the urge to write, but being constantly on the move makes it difficult. I have written numerous articles. Also my time is too taken up with building-construction responsibilities and meetings. I write almost entirely in Korean except for the overseas assignments.

On 25 September 1992 I helped to inaugurate the Institute of the Islamic Studies in Seoul, and Vivienne Stacey was the special guest lecturer for the occasion. She has played a significant role for the Institute and for its development.

Upper-room Evangelistic Association

From September 1996 I have been the Director-General of the Upper-room Evangelistic Association which the late Dr Helen Kim started with her great vision for evangelization of the whole nation and for unity interdenominationally. The Association was started in 1960. It started under a woman's leadership and ever since then the tradition of women's leadership has been maintained. It is self-supporting. All the members give money and time for mission, including the staff. No-one is paid for labour. The Association is interdenominational and has two purposes – prayer and evangelism. It aims exclusively to reach the poorest of the poor in the country as well as beyond its boundaries. In 1998 twenty-three local teams were sent out to help weak rural churches in Korea and seven overseas teams to India, China, Philippines, the Middle East, Japan and Africa. Diverse groups meet regularly each week for fellowship, for teaching, for mission training, and for the Governing Board which consists of about a hundred members.

Preaching

Other ministries include preaching in Urdu for Pakistanis in Seoul at the Onnuri Church (Onnuri means 'all nations'). Who would have ever thought that I could still speak Urdu, having left Pakistan in 1974 for good? I have been preaching once a month regularly for a group of Pakistani young men. I was recently invited to give a word of exhortation for its first worship service where the famous pastor, Ha, preached. I was present to translate his English sermon into Urdu. I welcomed the group in Urdu and gave a testimony. Having seen the response from the group, the pastor on the spot invited me to preach every Sunday. I am thankful that I have this opportunity to meet and teach them the Scriptures in Urdu. God is merciful and gracious to me. I receive more than I give when I preach in Urdu.

Preaching in Southwark Cathedral in London (near London Bridge) where, I was told, Chaucer worshipped and Shakespeare used to drop in, was an experience for me. I was invited by the Church Missionary Society (now Church Mission Society) to be the speaker for its 192nd annual assembly. My sermon, printed by the CMS, was entitled 'Press On'. Bishop Michael Nazir-Ali told me that I was the second woman preacher in 192 years. I spoke from a Korean context. (Dr Michael Nazir-Ali, now

Bishop of Rochester in the UK, had been appointed a PFES staff worker in 1968.)

Reflections on pluralism and mission

It is 17 July 1998, Constitution Day, a public holiday in Korea, which commemorates fifty years since the constitution was accepted. As I teach in a religiously pluralistic society (Korea has at least four major religious traditions which have been continuing for 5,000 years), I have to encounter the issue of pluralism and mission. Broadly, it is essential for Christians to live peacefully as peacemakers with people of other faiths. There should be a spirit of co-operation regardless of their religious convictions about the problems of poverty, ecology, health, unification and education. These national issues are the concern of all Koreans regardless of their religious convictions. Christians should take the initiative in all these issues based on the biblical teaching of love. A clear presentation of Jesus Christ as Lord and Saviour is needed in speech, in writing, in the media and in life. The proclamation of the gospel cannot be replaced by anything else. The Scriptures, the Bible, should be taught in culturally relevant ways so that people can understand the core of the message and apply it to their lives and be changed by the work of the Holy Spirit. I have come to think that we Christians assume too easily that what we say and do convey the message of the gospel, but often people hear differently and misunderstand. Somehow, it should be our life which speaks strongly of who Jesus is and what his salvation means. In this there is an inevitable process, which never ends: the process of repentance. In spite of the reality of the very pious life of some people of other faiths, it is not a help at all to think that all faiths lead to one and the same way. It is a very difficult task to meet my students and teach the uniqueness of Jesus, as often it seems there is no difference among peoples of different faith convictions. The uniqueness of Jesus Christ must be communicated more meaningfully to peoples in Korea and, for that matter, to other peoples in Asia. Personally, I am drawn more than ever before to Jesus Christ as the healer and peacemaker in this torn and suffering world. He is the crucified and living one in this world. How can I communicate this reality of two seemingly conflicting truths of being dead and living in this world?

Vivienne continues

Some of Chae Ok's translation work

Two years after the murder of our former UBTC student Esther John in 1960, Chae Ok translated the English booklet on Esther's life into Korean. She also translated Isobel Kuhn's book *By Searching* in 1971. She translated in 1975 *Asian Mission Studies: A Review* and an *Appraisal of the All-Asia Mission Consultation*, and in 1976 *New Resources for World Evangelization*.

Institute of Islamic Studies, Seoul

The Republic of Korea gives us an example of how a Muslim minority was established in a country which had no Korean Muslims. In 1955 two Turks with the UN Forces started to preach. The four stages of Islamic growth, as outlined by the Muslims, have been: the introductory stage, the preparatory stage, the settled stage, and finally the take-off stage. There are now more than 33,000 Korean Muslims. The mosque in Seoul stocks the Korea Muslim Federation booklet *Islam in Korea*, from which this information is taken. The Korean church needs to meet its Muslim neighbours and to know more about Islam. There are now mosques in six major cities. Islam is very much on the increase in Korea. As Korea is monocultural, short-term experiences in Pakistan, Bangladesh and Egypt are particularly useful for Korean Christians planning to work in the Middle East or other Muslim areas.[1]

The inauguration of the Institute of Islamic Studies took place in September 1992 with the backing of church leaders, notably Dr Chun Chae Ok, Dr Gweon Hgung-Ki and Andrew Narm (formerly General Secretary of KIVCF and Interserve, Korea). Its literature, papers, information, lectures, short courses, library and research facilities are designed for South East Asia as well as for Korea. One hopes that the Institute will be a place of Christian prayer for Muslims as well as a place for interchange with Muslims. So far its activities have included research on Christian–Muslim relationships, publication of an annual journal, an annual open lecture, ten week-long seminars, monthly study groups, training of researchers, networking with other international institutes concerned with Islamic studies, and co-operation with mission societies. The Institute of Islamic Studies in Seoul, for which she personally donated the land, will indeed be a significant part of Dr Chun Chae Ok's legacy.

Chapter 5

Antonia Leonora van der Meer

Vivienne introduces Antonia (Tonica)

In 1983 at the IFES General Committee in the UK I heard an Angolan Christian (Dr Filipe Matuba, as I discovered sixteen years later from Tonica) talk for two minutes about the sufferings of his country. I decided to pray for him and Angola every time I heard Angola mentioned. Then in 1987 I met Tonica in Bogatá, Columbia. She was a Brazilian who had been working since 1984 for IFES in Angola with Grupos Bíblicos de Estudantes Cristãos de Angola. I admired her courage. Twelve years later, in early 1999, I went to Brazil to interview Tonica at the Evangelical Center for Missions in Viçosa, where she is living, engaged in training young professionals who are preparing to work in cross-cultural situations. Angola was still much on her heart, and she was planning a short return visit.

Tonica tells her story

Childhood and early years

I was born on 24 October 1945 into a Christian family in
Brazil. My mother came to Brazil with her parents and
grandparents in 1913 at the age of two. The first settlers came
in 1910 because of difficulties in supporting their families in the
weak economy of the Netherlands. They had responded to an
invitation by British Railways and the Brazilian Government to
build railways. Each family received a piece of land, a simple,
small house, and two cows. Eventually everything was to be
paid for. My mother did not revisit her home country until she
was sixty-five.

My father, also from the Netherlands, was the youngest of a
poor family. He was bright, and the family struggled hard so
that he could finish a teacher-training course. He wanted to be a
missionary, but there was no finance for further training. He
came to Brazil in 1936, as a teacher for immigrant children.
This seemed like half-way to becoming a missionary. Ahead of
him, one of my mother's uncles, with more education than the
others, had become a teacher and administrator of a small co-
operative, and leader of the church which had existed for many
years without a pastor. A Lutheran pastor came occasionally to
baptize children, and to celebrate holy communion. The
immigrants were from various Reformed churches. After some
initial difficulties they formed a united church, called the
Evangelical Reformed Church.

There were seven children in our family. First came all the
girls, of whom I was the second. When I was four, I already had
two younger sisters, and after a few weeks a baby brother. This
meant many joys to share, plenty of friends to play with, but
also competition and fighting between us.

My father was the only one in the community who was strict

about starting school at the correct age. I studied in a very big class (many of them had repeated one or two years), and most were three to five years older than me. I was good at studying and loved it, and got better marks than most of them, but I was very bad at drawing and sports, probably because I was much younger and I felt very clumsy. My sisters (who were in smaller classes) were always the first in their classes, and I was only the third or the fourth. Every month my father would say something about that (probably just joking), but I started to feel dumb and unintelligent. My father was very strict, and demanded unquestioning obedience. I never obeyed unquestioningly; I wanted to understand things. I wanted him to speak to me and treat me as a person. So I was a stubborn little girl and often got a spanking.

Our church, like our Christian life at home, was very formal. The pastor or an elder always prayed and preached in the church, and at home father always read the Bible and prayed after lunch and supper. We learned little prayers to use before meals and before sleeping. As a child I trusted the Lord and knew he was good and cared for me, but during my teens I became rebellious. I had some serious health problems for some years with the continuing threat of becoming blind. After a succession of five deaths (two uncles, two aunts and my grandfather) in our very close-knit extended family, I started to feel that Jesus had lived two thousand years ago, and God was very far away in heaven, and what about us now?

Once I went to see the pastor to tell him I wasn't sure that I belonged to Jesus or that I would go to heaven.

'Don't you believe the Bible is true? Don't you believe Jesus is God's Son?' he asked.

'Yes, I do.'

'Then don't be silly, creating problems in your mind.'

I left, feeling discouraged, and thought that maybe being a Christian is just that: trying to be good, accepting some truths, and seeing what might happen when we die. But I was bothered about all the social and spiritual problems I saw around me. Surely God must have to do with them. There were many joys as well; we had loving uncles and aunts. My mother was very patient, and worked day and night to serve us. She cooked, baked, cleaned, made our clothes, and was always ready to listen and to explain things. We had plenty of space to play, to discover the beautiful things of nature – woods, waterfalls, climbing precipices and trees, collecting lovely flowers.

How I came to Christ and joined ABU

In the country, only five years of schooling were available. Some youngsters went to study at Catholic colleges, but my father was afraid we would be influenced by their doctrine. Others studied at an evangelical school, but for some years they had poor leadership and severe problems in discipline, so, in spite of my requests, there were no further studies.

Years later we discovered a special programme offered by the Brazilian government. Students over eighteen could attend an evening course and do exams twice a year. If successful, they could then do seven years of schooling in two years. I did these courses while I worked part-time, and studied very hard, managing to finish in two years. Entry examinations for the university were very hard, but as a cousin was doing her exam I decided to go with her. So I got there! Incredible! I was a university student. I was very happy, and continued to live completely for my studies, starting to have some dreams about a career as a university teacher.

In a big family the natural thing was to start working as soon as possible to support oneself and help the family. Although I was at the university, I continued to work. Being so concerned with my studies, I didn't bother about what I ate. I became ill. The doctor said it was poor nutrition, so I started to take better care of my body, but I had very little time for relaxation and sports. I lived with friends from Dutch-background families from the countryside. One of them repeatedly invited me to Bible studies arranged by the ABU, the IFES-affiliated movement in Brazil. She kept saying how good student camps were, so I decided to go during the summer holidays in January 1970. I travelled for twenty-four hours by bus to Goiânia, expecting a lot of fun and swimming. There was a lot of fun, but I soon discovered that people had a different way of speaking about and relating to God. It all seemed very strange. People had 'quiet times', so I would climb in a tree and read my Bible as well. Later, in small groups, some people said, 'The Lord spoke to me this morning.' I would look at them and think, 'How can the Lord have spoken to her? I didn't hear any powerful voice coming from heaven.' When they asked me about my relationship with the Lord I didn't really understand what they were talking about.

One evening there was a special prayer time instead of the scheduled lecture. Starting at 7:30pm, it just went on, without anybody noticing the time. People were pouring out their hearts before God. I thought, 'Oh! If only I could pray like that, but I can't.' I managed to keep quiet for more than three hours. Then I couldn't any more, and opened my heart and mouth as well, and just said what was on my heart. Suddenly life seemed very different. I had a tremendous sense of being overwhelmed by God's love, poured out on me. When I arrived, I had felt ashamed to tell people I worked as a saleswoman, which was considered an inferior kind of job for a university student. So I told them I worked in an office. Suddenly that didn't matter at all, and I told people, 'You know, I didn't tell you the truth, but I work as a saleswoman, and not in an office.' It was completely unimportant, but telling the truth became important. I was released from my feeling of inferiority, and the last days of the camp were some of the happiest of my life.

Returning home I just sat there telling my family and friends for as long as they cared to listen. When I returned to my job and classes I did the same thing. Soon I became one of the leaders of ABU in Curitiba. I learned to lead Bible studies and went to other camps. We were a small local group, but very united, and we became great friends. One university colleague came back from his holidays talking of his new experience of personal faith in Christ, so we could support each other in our witness.

After a year and a half I was invited to work at the Dutch Embassy in Brasília. I was dreaming of becoming a university lecturer, and the diplomatic life didn't really attract me. I asked the ABU group to pray with me. One of them asked, 'Couldn't it be that the Lord wants you to go to Brasília? I know they are trying to develop student ministry, but nobody has enough experience and you may be a help.' I couldn't forget this question and kept thinking, 'If the Lord wants me to go, I can't possibly refuse.' So I went, and for three years worked at the Embassy, finished my studies and helped with student work in Brasilia, Goiânia, and Anápolis. Convinced that it was time to leave the Embassy, I worked part-time with Wycliffe Bible Translators, as a secretary, and part-time with ABU, for the next two years.

Information on Aliança Bíblica Universitária do Brasil

The Brazilian student movement started in 1957 through the ministry of people from the InterVarsity Christian Fellowship of the USA and Canada. They shared their vision for student work with Brazilian students. Ruth Siemens worked as an English language teacher in Curitiba for several years, investing time in people. Another pioneer, Robert Young, would eat only bananas (very cheap in Brazil) on one or two days a week so that he could use the money saved for student work. He was a visionary, sharing his vision with first-generation student leaders. Dr Ross Douglas from Canada came as a university teacher in physics. He and his wife Elaine adapted well to the Brazilian scene. Eventually, he became a Brazilian citizen. For many years they were very strong and consistent supporters of Brazilian student work.

I did not meet these pioneers during those early years, but I had the special joy of meeting Ruth Siemens at the Lausanne II Congress in Manila, Philippines, in 1989. She has been involved in facilitating tentmaking ministries, investigating opportunities, and leading candidates to the right contacts.

Next came Wayne Bragg (USA), the first General Secretary of ABU, who found Neuza Itioka, the first national staff worker who succeeded him in the early 1970s. Neuza was a very dynamic and able leader, good at discovering people with gifts and engaging them in the ministry. Through Neuza I became a staff worker, although I never thought I was capable of such ministry. ABU grew and expanded. New staff workers were engaged, and in 1976 the national leadership passed from Neuza to four male leaders, of whom Dieter Brepohl was General Secretary (until 1985) and Valdir Steuernagel was Assistant General Secretary. The number of staff grew very quickly. Student work expanded, reaching more and more colleges and schools all over the country.

From 1983 we went through a bad crisis. The political climate was changing, and a group of active staff and student leaders became Marxist, rejecting anybody who wasn't as not a real Christian. Dieter was rejected because he came from a wealthy family. ABU had always questioned the *status quo* of the military regime much more than most of the evangelical churches that expounded Romans 12 to defend their position of complete unquestioning submission to this dictatorship. For a few years every staff decision-making meeting was very painful. Heavy accusations were voiced and a lot of bitterness developed.

Thanks to God, the troublemakers eventually left the movement, but it was much weakened. We lost support from evangelical churches and many groups had stopped functioning. Dieter was invited to become IFES Regional Secretary of Latin America, and served well from 1985 to 1998. Ziel Machado, the new General Secretary of ABU, was still very young, but dynamic, faithful and wise. He worked discreetly, ready to listen to all, without compromising, and slowly the movement came back on track and started to grow again. Ziel was succeeded by Ricardo Wesley Borges, again a very young but committed leader.

The Brazilian student work was usually strong in evangelism, though there always were groups more concerned with the preservation of their private faith in an evil world. Missionary vision resulted in the first Latin American Mission Conference in 1976, in Curitiba, with more than five hundred students. A team of staff was chosen to develop holistic mission vision and practice. Paul Freston, an Englishman well adjusted to Brazil, contributed greatly with a critical analysis of the witness of Brazilian evangelicals in politics. Iolanda Freston (his Brazilian wife), Rubens Osório and Jadyr Elon Moreira Braga were the other team members. As a result several social projects were started in Brazil. Some of them still continue, as the following example demonstrates.

A group of medical students started to pray about serving in a very poor region of Brazil where no medical help was available. They started a hospital in Córrego do Ouro in Goiás. It was very isolated; not even a newspaper was available in the town. They served very well, earning love and respect. I spent a week with them, with a team of students from Brasilia, doing door-to-door evangelism and preaching in the main square. As a result, a Baptist church was planted. Two of these doctors, Credival and Raquel, later went to a more needy town in Rondonia (in the far north), and started offering medical help to the poor. After fifteen years, Raquel was invited to stand as a candidate for the office of a town councillor. She said, 'All right, but I won't have time to campaign.' Nevertheless she got the most votes. Another of our former staff workers, Wasny de Roure, married to a faithful ABU student, was very concerned with politics. He is now a member of the National Congress in Brasilia and is known for his ethical conduct, incorruptibility and social concern.

Through ABU missionary vision some of the conference members in 1976 became missionaries in Italy and Angola. A Bolivian, Marcelo Vargas, who became a Christian through the ministry of ABU in Brazil, was sent back to Bolivia with Brazilian support to work with Felicity Houghton in starting a student ministry. ABU also received four students from Guinea Bissau, assuming responsibility for them, while their support came mainly through World Vision. Two of them were engaged. Brandão Gomes Có studied medicine and his future wife Leandra trained as a nurse. He holds key positions in the medical scene of his country. Benjamim Lomba, a very active and dynamic Christian, became a lawyer.

Seven hundred people from all over Latin America gathered for a student conference in Bolivia, in January 1998, celebrating forty years of IFES as a Latin American movement. It was a time of reflection on our history and present witness, and a time to renew our missionary vision and commitment. In the Bible studies on Revelation we studied the church at Ephesus, which lost its first love. Our commitment was renewed as we humbled ourselves before the Lord, confessing our sins as individuals and as national movements.

The ABU publishing department grew and became very respected in Brazil, Angola, Mozambique and Portugal. One Angolan pastor who didn't know I had any links with ABU told me, 'If a book comes from ABU Editora you can trust that it is serious and very good.' It printed The Bible Speaks Today series, some good books written by former staff, some C. S. Lewis books and quite a few of John Stott's books.

My calling to a wider ministry

For the first ever ABU mission conference held in Latin America in 1976, 3,000 students wishing to participate were required to do a correspondence course. Only the best 500 were selected to come. I was involved in writing the guides for personal prayer times and Bible studies. During this conference a British/ Canadian missionary, Dennis Pape, kept insisting, 'You Brazilians are responsible for Angola, Mozambique and Guinea Bissau. They receive help from the communist countries. Europeans and Americans can't go, but you will be welcome.' I agreed, but understood that this was for the darker Brazilians. I was obviously much too white to go as a missionary to Africa. I would remind them of all the exploitation by the colonial powers.

In 1977 I accepted the invitation to become secretary at the ABU headquarters in São Paulo, and continued to work as a travelling secretary. I began studies at the Baptist Theological Faculty. At a weekly prayer group of students and staff we prayed for ABU, for the world's needs, for the nations and for missionary needs. We forgot the time and usually prayed through the night. This increased my longing to become a missionary. In 1979 I travelled alone from Recife to São Paulo (fifty-two hours by bus), to think and pray and finally decide what I should be doing next. I prayed for the opportunity to receive good training. A few weeks later some friends invited me to tea to meet Martin Goldsmith, a lecturer at All Nations Christian College in the UK. After hearing from him about the college I decided that it was the place for me.

Despite lack of finance for my studies I applied to ANCC and the Lord provided. In the period 1980 to 1982 I became finally convinced that the Lord wanted me to go to Africa, and that he knew very well that I was white but it didn't matter to him; he would go with me. I also discovered I had skin cancer and my doctor said I couldn't possibly become a missionary in a very warm climate. For a time this health condition was depressing. When I returned to Brazil in 1982 I found a Christian specialist who gave me good treatment and advice (refusing any payment). He encouraged me to go to Africa if I learned to protect myself from the sun.

In 1981 I took part in the Formación Conference of IFES in Oxford, and for two years was very involved with foreign students in Oxford. St Aldate's became my church in the UK. I organized Bible study groups for foreign students, in English and Spanish.

In 1982 I offered my services to ABU again, while I was waiting for clear guidance about the future. They accepted me with the warning, 'We can't promise you any salary; we are in a very difficult situation.' I accepted the challenge, and I never lacked the necessary support. In 1983 our General Secretary, Dieter Brepohl, went to the IFES General Committee in the UK and met Dr Filipe Matuba, from Angola, who was imploring Brazil for help for the student groups he was starting in Angola. When I received this specific invitation I knew that this was what I had been waiting for. So I made my first journey to Angola in March 1984.

Background information on Angola

Angola, with its capital Luanda and a population of eleven million, is on the west coast of Africa, just north of Namibia, and south of the Congos. The Portuguese arrived in Angola in 1492.

Independence did not come until 1975. The Portuguese had tried to keep control of Angola by maintaining a low level of studies for the Africans and making further education almost impossible for them. The few Angolans with any further education had received it abroad through evangelical missions, so most of the revolutionary leaders came from evangelical families. The Portuguese government, concluding that missionaries were the instigators of rebellion, started to persecute evangelical Christians. Portugal itself was passing through a crisis and political revolution, so it finally decided to hand back government to its colonies. In Angola several groups were fighting for independence. One such was the MPLA (Popular Movement for the Liberation of Angola) with a Marxist ideology, from the north, which started its struggle in 1961. Looking for support from outside, the MPLA found a willing Soviet Union and Cuba, and so sent leaders to these countries for further training. When the Portuguese left, the MPLA decided to proclaim itself the new national government. This caused a number of civil wars. Another group was the FNLA from still further north (from the Bakongo people), mixed with people from the Democratic Republic of the Congo. People from the north had been crossing the border and many had spent half of their lives in that country speaking poor Portuguese with a French accent. They were too foreign to the Angolans, and eventually stopped their fight, but are still a political party. The third group, UNITA (National Union for the Total Independence of Angola), from the south, started with help from China. They decided to switch and became anti-communist and so received plenty of support from the USA and the Republic of South Africa, with very good military training and arms. They started to fight as soon as the country became independent.

From 1975 to 1991 this war continued, spreading ever more widely over the country. It was mostly guerrilla warfare but with some attacks on cities. The roads became very dangerous. Many mines were planted. Usually no records of them were kept. At one time there were more mines than people in Angola. Life limped along in the cities, and people would flee from the countryside to the cities to keep alive. As their fields were also mined, farming became very dangerous, and hunger increased. As a result of stepping on mines, or through shrapnel or bullets, Angola has a very great number of handicapped people – at least 100,000, who have lost one or both legs.

Angola is a rich country with much fertile land. For a time it exported coffee, rice, corn, fish and fruit. The riches from oil and diamond mines didn't benefit ordinary people. In the war from 1992 to 1994 the people who lived nearest the diamond mines were starving, and had no medical care. Most of the revenues from the mines and oil were spent on armaments. The Marxist government wasn't too harsh in persecuting Christians, but there were restrictions. From 1991 things started to change; Angola became more democratic, with religious freedom. A Marxist economy was replaced by capitalism, enriching a few and making the majority even poorer.

The Christian student organization was called Grupos Bíblicos de Estudantes Cristãos de Angola (GBECA).

Finally, I went to Angola

My family had always supported my work with ABU but didn't agree with my going to Angola. The subject was taboo; I couldn't speak about it. But when I went to say goodbye, my mother and my brother, who is a pastor, gave their blessing.

Arriving in Angola was not very romantic or exciting. The airport was extremely hot, with long queues, no taxi service, and, after several years, only one available telephone. There was only one very expensive hotel. Suddenly two Brazilian brothers in Christ materialized, welcoming me. They worked in Angola, having a desire to see the church grow. One of them took me home. The capital city, Luanda, was very poor, and everywhere one saw armed soldiers, some of whom were very drunk. The public squares had army tanks instead of flowers. It was a depressing scene, and during the first weeks I was frightened to walk on the streets.

I soon met the small group of students in Luanda. We started prayer meetings and training sessions for leaders. I also shared with key Christian leaders about the goals of student work, from the point of view of IFES. Many had doubts. One church, having received a missionary linked with another student movement, became unhappy with him, and people linked to IFES were considered to be in the same category as those who wouldn't submit to local leadership, thereby creating problems in the churches. The churches of the Association of Evangelicals, which had invited me, also held this view. After some months of fellowship, they invited me to their General Assembly, where they asked me many questions, and then decided that they would trust me. So I was invited to return to Angola. The first General Secretary of the Council of Christian Churches received me very cordially. His successor considered us too narrow-minded in always wanting to study the Bible when there was so much valuable literature about. He was followed by a leader who has always supported us.

Dr Filipe Matuba, who had become a Christian through the ministry of a Swiss GBU couple in Kinshasa, where he studied medicine, was the founder of the student movement in Angola. He came from Lubango, in the south, to invite me to come and meet the first and strongest of the student groups so far. My first experience with national flights wasn't easy, even though he had friends working with the air company. After spending twelve hours in a very hot place, without water, food, toilet or anything available, we managed to travel on the same day. (I never again travelled without taking a bottle of water with me). Lubango is a nice city with a pleasant climate; there were flowers around and I soon felt at home, and became a great friend of the

Matuba children. I started having meetings with the students, and prepared training materials, making stencilled copies to leave with them. I enjoyed fellowship at the church, learned to appreciate Angolan food, and met a few expatriate missionaries.

After a few weeks I had to return to Luanda to renew my visa. It took three weeks of hard work to get a visa for three months. The AEA (Evangelical Alliance of Angola) office had only an office boy at the time and I personally had to walk to the Foreign Office to get forms (forty minutes' walk and some steep hills in the hot sun), type them, walk to the house of the Vice-President (forty minutes' walk in another direction), and walk again to the Foreign Office. After a few days I was told that everything was wrong, and started the whole process again, with the same results. After handing in the papers for the sixth time I got my visa. In the meantime I was also having meetings with students, visiting churches, and getting integrated. Eventually, after special prayer, I lost my fear of walking about.

My next journey was to Huambo, a central southern city, a very pleasant-looking place, but already much plagued by the war. It took several days at the airport to get a plane. This became the norm. At first I felt embarrassed that other people had to get up before dawn to get me to the airport, but I learned that interdependence was essential for survival, and that people served each other without questioning. I was welcomed by the Baptist pastor Adelino Chilundulu, who had just received two missionary ladies from Brazil. The three of us shared the rooms above the church. On our first night there was a terrible fight nearby. Some houses were destroyed by bombs. There was a lot of machine-gun fire, and everything trembled – I even more than the walls. I went to the next room, and the three of us prayed for the rest of the night, very frightened indeed. I was very well received, but it was a time of hunger. The three of us shared meals with the pastor's family. With very little food, we were hungry during the whole day. I would dream during the night that I was going to eat, and would awake just as I was about to take the first bite, feeling very hungry.

I started to visit pastors and churches. We organized a special meeting where I would present the vision for student work. The church was crowded, as they received so few foreign visitors. The message was well received, and soon we started our first meetings. At an early meeting on 'How to share the gospel with your friends' a non-Christian became convinced and wanted to commit his life to Christ. Despite initial difficulties I left Huambo after a month, leaving behind a functioning student group, under enthusiastic leadership.

I spent time in Lubango again, and in Luanda, but the time to return to Brazil came too quickly. I returned to visit my family and shared about the spiritual hunger and receptivity of the Angolan people, about their amazing hospitality, about the Lord's blessings, and how the Lord changed their hearts. From then onwards my parents, brothers and sisters, uncles and aunts and cousins supported my ministry, taking an interest and finding joy in helping with my support and in sending Bibles and clothes to Angola.

Getting my visa took fifteen months. A new General Secretary of the Association of Evangelicals was elected after six months. He wrote to tell me not come as there was no place where I could live. No flats were available for rent. I wrote to many of the friends I had made, and to him saying, 'I am not asking for a flat. If anyone has a room where I can live, I will be happy. If there is no room, I will share a room with other people. I am sure the Lord wants me to come.' I received a lot of negative answers: 'Sadly, sister, there is no room for you.' This was true; due to the war the cities were crowded. It was normal to have four families (up to thirty people) sharing a two-bedroom flat. Good friends started to question my wanting to return to Angola. 'Why don't you go and work somewhere else?'

But I was convinced of the Lord's leading. Finally Pastor Chilundulu from Huambo invited me to stay with them until some place would be found in Luanda. After a few more months I got my visa and was ready to return.

Living in Angola

I arrived in Luanda and was received by Pastor Octavio Fernando, the General Secretary of the AEA. He had good news. The previous evening, visiting a sister from the church, he had lamented, 'Tomorrow our missionary is coming and we haven't found any housing for her.'

The lady answered, 'My daughter works on a petrol exploration station, and spends three weeks a month away from her flat. She needs somebody to look after the flat because the present tenant is moving back to her home town.'

So I had somewhere to go. It was a good place to live, very central, a building in better condition than most of the others. Sometimes the lift worked, sometimes it stuck when you were in it. Sometimes water came in through the taps during the night. I would leave the taps open. If I heard any water dripping, I would get up and fill every bucket with water, because nobody knew when it would come again; maybe it would be months.

I worked during the mornings at the office of the Association of Evangelicals, helping with correspondence, producing a bulletin, translating international correspondence and interpreting for visitors. The General Secretary was a leader with vision, and slowly the AEA grew, serving the churches. I helped to restore the concept that social action is part of the ministry of the church. I also helped to establish contacts with Christian organizations abroad.

The Angolan church felt forgotten, and received very little support of any kind, until I travelled with the General Secretary to Europe in 1987. We made contacts in the UK, the Netherlands and Germany, and from then onwards we started to receive some help.

It was difficult to get our papers ready (always a lot of bureaucracy). We needed the Director of the Angolan Air Company to sign one more paper, urgently. But his secretary said, 'Sorry, but this week he won't be at his office; he is working with the minister, and will return to normal work next week.'

Pastor Octavio insisted, and the lady said, 'All right, you come on Friday, but I won't promise anything.'

He came back discouraged, but we decided to fast and pray the next day (Tuesday) and that he would return on Wednesday. When he entered the office again the secretary was all smiles, and said, 'But I told you yesterday that everything was in order.'

'But I wasn't here yesterday. I came on Monday.'

'Oh! No, you were here yesterday! Look in my book.'

There was the name of Pastor Octavio, who supposedly had come and solved the problems while we had been praying and fasting. It was a clever angel, obviously, with a good Angolan accent.

When I left Angola, the AEA had grown and become quite strong. At first there was a very small office, rented, with barely enough room for three people. When I left they had several buildings, good office space, room for visitors, and some houses belonging to the AEA. The General Secretary of the AEA of Africa came to a conference in 1994 and reported that the Angolan Association was one of the strongest ones in all Africa.

Student work with GBECA

Student work continued with one or two visits to each province a year, at first to Lubango and Huambo. Soon Benguela/Lobito (twin cities on the central southern coast) also invited me and developed an active student ministry among high-school students. In 1986 things at first went smoothly, but then pressure started to build up against Christian student groups. An American with a big camera went around taking pictures in the middle of a war situation. The police followed him and observed with whom he stayed. They confiscated his films at the airport and started to persecute the people who had been in contact with him. This created a greater prejudice against the churches. Dr Filipe was harassed, and he felt so oppressed that he burned almost all the papers I had left for the students.

The group in Lubango asked me not to come in 1987. 'When you arrive at the airport they know you have come. It is not the right moment.'

'All right. You tell me when to come, and I will wait and we will pray.'

The faithful remnant of eight students were called three times to choose between their studies or their faith – twice privately, but the third time in a big public meeting. They said, 'We want to serve our country faithfully, but we cannot deny our Saviour.' So when the new school year started in October, their names were listed, saying that they weren't allowed to continue their studies, and the leader was put in prison. The same night people came to their houses forcing them to enter the army. José Bernardo Luacute, known as Zeca, the present General Secretary, escaped because he is partially lame. The Angolan doctor wanted to approve him anyway, but the Russian doctor insisted that he was unfit. All the others had several official reasons not to be in the army. Some were already older than thirty; some had other deficiencies; all were working for the government as teachers. They were taken and sent at first to Luanda (accused of being politically dangerous), and then to several different provinces.

Some people advised against my visiting them in Luanda, but I insisted and went with some Angolan friends. The soldiers at the gate denied knowing anything about students who had come from Lubango. We mentioned that they were religious young men, and after some more talking one of the soldiers said, 'Ah! It's the ones who have been singing!' So the soldier went and brought them. We had some beautiful moments of fellowship and prayer at the gate. I felt reassured by their faith and courage.

After two years the accusations against them were withdrawn and they returned, free to study and work. Zeca had been told, 'If you don't say anything and keep quiet, we will allow you to continue your studies.'

He answered, 'I will not return before my brothers have come back. I will fight that justice may be done.'

So he presented papers to several authorities, with the support of the General Secretary of the AEA and his church leaders. After a long time the government moved the Director of the college to a governmental position in another province, and withdrew any accusation against them. The imprisoned brother was interrogated for days, for many hours, with heavy accusations. A letter against the government was produced, apparently in his handwriting. By God's grace he was a very respected teacher of the Portuguese language, and the person imitating his handwriting had made very basic mistakes in spelling, which eventually were accepted as proof of forgery. After a few months he was released, but had to appear subdued, because he was still very much under observation.

The Communist Party was very strong in Benguela/Lobito and had extensive control over the churches. Whenever I arrived about a hundred very eager young people came (many walking for hours), wanting to learn as much as I could give them. During meals or free times I would have a few of them around me asking more questions, hardly giving me time to rest. Only a few pastors had any training, and at school their faith was being questioned. Evangelical books weren't available. I started to take them some books, which I bought with my salary in

Brazil and sold to a few of the keen readers. To them I was like a 'walking Christian encyclopaedia'.

Once I was asked to speak about 'Philosophy and Christian faith'. Knowing that they meant Marxist philosophy, I borrowed some of their books to read, and some Christian books as well. This talk was planned for Sunday afternoon in a big, very simple and crowded church. One minute before I had to speak a note was passed to me saying that the Director of Religious Affairs was present. He was in charge of controlling the churches. I prayed very much for wisdom during my talk and the question time afterwards. Then tea was served to visitors and I found myself sitting next to this director. He thanked me, saying that he had learned a lot from me. I was very surprised. We continued to talk, and later he said that he was still a materialist, but certainly no longer an atheist.

After 1991 things started to open up, and slowly new opportunities for witnessing to students at their residence halls, and even at the university, occurred. January 1995 marked a special event. Two visitors from Brazil, Dr Ross Douglas and a student, Marcos Augusto, came on a visit. The Rector of the university and directors of colleges received them. Doors were wide open for lectures on science and Christian faith (a very attractive subject in a society influenced by Marxist philosophy).

Ministry in the hospitals

In 1984 in Luanda, some friends invited me to visit a hospital with them. I went, and fell in love with this ministry of encouragement, evangelism and practical service to those people so very hurt by the war. When I returned in 1985, this work had stopped. After some months of making contacts, I found a few friends who wanted to start it again with me. After I left, some teenager friends continued this ministry.

We visited the Centre for Rehabilitation and Physical

Medicine, where the patients were either lame or had lost legs or arms. Later on we visited the main hospital, and for some time the military hospital as well. People were desperately hurt. They suffered from hunger and a lack of most basic commodities (like soap and towels), and were very lonely and hopeless. They loved receiving visits. Some were so open that they wanted to become Christians on the first visit. Many knew too little about God, Jesus and the Bible, and it took them several months to understand the message well enough to make a response. Others were Marxists and didn't want to believe, but barriers started to come down through friendship, and many came to faith. The fact that most stayed in the hospital for months or even years gave an opportunity for more teaching.

I can tell many beautiful and many sad stories. One is about José Gomes, a young man who became tetraplegic at sixteen years of age through a diving accident. After a long time he arrived at the hospital in a bad state. As a Marxist he thought the Bible was for ignorant people. His mother came from the province to help him, but she had never lived in a city and was run down by a car and died a few months later. José was desperately sad. I became his friend during this time, and after a few months he started to ask questions about the Bible. I encouraged these questions and after a few more months he was convinced enough to want to believe. He became a Christian and changed completely, becoming very happy and full of life and joy. People coming to the hospital stopped at his bed and he had a word of encouragement for all. He read Joni Eareckson's book *Joni* and decided that he wanted to learn to write with his mouth like her. He started to train, and after some time he wrote a beautiful poem and gave it to me. I encouraged him to write more. Later I suggested that he should write his own life story and I typed it for him. Its second edition was printed in Brazil. He also started to design notelets with Christian messages.

Why I returned to Brazil

I agreed with the IFES philosophy of autonomous student movements, and that most staff should be as close as possible in age to the students, so I knew I wasn't invited or sent to a lifelong ministry. From 1991 I started to receive letters from the General Secretary of IFES and from the Regional Secretary of English and Portuguese-speaking Africa asking how long I still needed to remain. I discussed this with the leaders of GBECA, and they suggested three more years. Eventually they asked me to stay another year, because the war of 1992 had caused a lot of havoc and many things had to be rebuilt. IFES agreed with this.

Once I met the Regional Secretary, David Zac Niringiye, a good friend who said, 'It is time for you to return to Brazil. You have done the most important thing in finding quality people to continue the ministry.'

'But what if I stayed in Angola with a different ministry?'

'No,' he said, with real love and respect. 'That is not right. People love you and respect you. If you stay they will run to you at the first crisis with the new leaders. You really have to leave.'

So I agreed. I left Angola in June 1995 as we had already found in Zeca a good national leader to continue the work, and my presence might even have hindered the transition period. But leaving Angola seemed like dying. It was very hard indeed. I still have a great desire to return eventually to Angola or to another African country, to serve for a number of years training national leaders and missionaries.

In Brazil I had received invitations over the years to become a teacher at the Evangelical Center for Missions in Viçosa, which has the specific vision of training tentmakers. I had become concerned at the struggles of many Brazilian missionary friends who hadn't received any missiological or transcultural training. It felt right to accept this invitation.

To work at CEM has been a joy. It is a small community

with usually twenty-two to twenty-four resident students doing a two-year training for transcultural ministry. We also offer a Master's degree in missiology, but such students usually come during the holidays for a few modules (subjects). We have forty-four former students working in twenty-one countries, with several Brazilian, Latin or international missions. Most have stayed on the field and work in Latin America and Africa. Several have gone to Muslim countries. There is a growing interest in ministry to Muslims. PMI International is a Latin mission to the Muslim world offering a good complementary training programme in Spain. Eleven of our students have started interdenominational or denominational mission training programmes in Ecuador, Peru, Bolivia and Spain, as well as in Brazil.

The Board of CEM agreed that I didn't need to belong fully to the Center, and indeed that it was advantageous for the institution if I had a wider ministry. So once a year I could go to Angola (or maybe Mozambique). In 1997 I went for five weeks, and taught at two seminaries in Huambo and Lubango and spent a week in Luanda, visiting student friends, families with whom I had special links, some churches and especially my needy handicapped friends, who were still going through very hard times.

About being single

I never decided that I didn't want to marry. I had a normal desire to marry and have children. But my calling was more important to me, and if my ministry would become impossible because of marrying somebody who didn't have the same vision, I knew I would feel great anguish. So I kept on praying and decided, 'I do not want to marry unless I meet somebody with the same calling and vision.'

I felt happy in my ministry, first in Brazil with ABU and later in Angola. Especially in Angola, being single helped me to live a very simple lifestyle, identifying with the nationals as much as possible, and to face risky places and times, because I knew what I was doing. I had chosen to serve the Lord in such a situation and felt peace about it. For mothers with children, war situations become much harder to cope with. So it was easier to be on my own. It also allowed me to travel more extensively and to have a wider ministry. Eventually I felt that singleness was the Lord's best for me.

It wasn't so easy in the Angolan context. Single women don't exist. If a woman is unhappy at not finding a husband just to herself, she will agree to become a second or third wife. The cultural pressure induces her to obtain respect as an adult female by producing a baby from a temporary relationship. To be a single mother is sad, but to be single and not a mother is much worse. In the church women had very little input anyhow. Sometimes I asked, 'Lord, what am I doing in this place?' But eventually I discovered that I had much more freedom to serve, exactly because of this lack of status. A male adult missionary was always perceived as a kind of threat to national leaders. How could I endanger anybody if I was just a woman, and a single, childless one at that?

But I had times when I struggled with loneliness, and when I felt very attracted to male friends. Once I had a dream that I was trying to climb a steep hill. It was very hard going and I wasn't progressing at all. Then I saw an old man, with a teenage boy who climbed the hill with quick, firm steps. I knew in my dream that they were Abraham and Isaac. A voice told me, 'You have to offer your Isaac as well.' And I knew I was meant to leave my desire for a husband in God's hands, and just rest in him, without regrets or questionings. It helped.

Chapter 6

Felicity Bentley-Taylor

Vivienne introduces Felicity

Ada Lum, who knows everyone, told me, 'Felicity is a woman of great simplicity in her lifestyle and focused ministry.' Ada met her once at Schloss Mittersill in Austria and next in Chile as well as several times in Europe and West Asia. 'She is very English, but people loved her.' Felicity and I first met at an inter-schools house party in North Wales in 1959. We next met twenty-four years later at the IFES General Committee in Ashburnham, UK, and then in Columbia in 1987, as well as in Wheaton, USA, at the IFES World Assembly in 1991. More recently I stayed with her and her husband, David, in their home in Hereford, UK, in August 1998.

Family and childhood

Stanley Houghton, Felicity's father, was the seventh of eight children, born to the Reverend Thomas Houghton and his wife in Bath in 1900. After leaving school, her father joined the staff of Monkton Combe Junior School, near Bath, studying at the same time to obtain his BA. During this period, God was calling him to go to China as a missionary.

At the age of twenty-six he sailed for China as a member of the China Inland Mission. He studied Chinese at the CIM language school, fully hoping to be assigned to work in a Chinese-speaking situation. But he was asked to join the staff of the Chefoo School on the northern coast of the province of Shandong.

In 1929 Felicity's mother, Dorothy Blanche Benson, a young woman of twenty-four, also sailed for China with the same missionary society. She was a primary-school teacher, and, after language study, was also designated to the staff of the Chefoo School. In fact, she and Stanley Houghton had already met in England and already felt drawn to one another. They recognized the answer to their prayers in the fact that both were sent to work in the same school. They were married there in January 1931. Stephen was born in October of the same year, Felicity Blanche on 14 November 1933, and Josephine in September 1936.

In 1881 Hudson Taylor had decided to found a Christian English-speaking school community to provide education for the children of CIM personnel working all over China, as well as for the children of business people who lived locally. The Houghtons' home was a semi-detached house in the compound that had developed around it and included more staff houses, the preparatory school, the coeducational secondary school, a boys' hostel and another for the girls, and a rest home, known as 'the San'. On leaving the gates of this compound, one crossed the road, stepped on to a spacious sandy beach and looked out over the waters of a large bay, as far as a promontory, known as the Bluff, on the horizon. The port and city of Chefoo lay to the west of the school. The city has expanded enormously in recent decades and is now known as Yantai.[1]

Felicity tells her story

The love of God and of our parents surrounded us from our earliest days. We imbibed the love of Christ and of his Word from the teaching and example of our parents. For this reason I cannot put a date to my conversion; rather, I can only marvel that God drew me to himself and revealed his Son to me as my Saviour and Lord through the steady Christian witness and training of my home and schooling.

While this was steady, the circumstances affecting my life as a child and young person were wholly destabilizing. When I was four, a life-and-death struggle broke out between China and Japan. Within two years, Japan obtained possession of most of China's ports. The province of Shandong fell into Japanese hands; soon the port of Chefoo was swarming with Japanese troops. Soldiers were posted at the gate of our compound. There they carried out their bayonet practice, accompanied by blood-curdling cries. I was frightened. The months between Pearl Harbour in December 1941 and November 1942 passed uneasily. We were no longer neutral citizens but enemies living in Japanese-occupied territory. Just before my ninth birthday, we lost our home and all it contained, except for what we could carry with us across the city, where the whole school was interned in four large houses once lived in by American Presbyterian missionaries. Now my parents, sister and I slept on top of boxes in one room which we shared with another family. A curtain divided their space from ours. My brother slept in a dorm with other boys in the same house.

Three good things I particularly connect with this strange period in our lives: a sudden sense of being filled with joy in God; learning to read the Bible every day on my own with the help of a schedule that covered the whole Bible in a year; and being drawn to the thought of following my parents' example and becoming a missionary teacher once I was of the age to do so. I asked my father what parts of the world were un-evangelized. What stuck in my mind from his answer was a reference to parts of South America. That became decisive for me, for from then on I set my face in the direction of a continent on the other side of the globe, from which I had never met anyone.

Another upheaval disrupted our life on Temple Hill, Chefoo, in the summer of the following year, 1943. The Japanese military authorities decided to have us transported by ship to Tsingatao and then by train to the interior of the province, to be integrated into the life of a much larger civilian internment camp of 1,400 internees from all over north-east China. Weihsien Camp became our next home until our liberation by American marines at the termination of the Second World War. In December 1945 we disembarked from a troopship in Southampton and went to stay with cousins we had not met before, and then with our grandfather Houghton, now a widower. We had come through an experience which was difficult for people in England to imagine, yet we on our part had little idea of what they had been through, having had practically no contact with anything or anybody outside the walls of our internment camp for almost three years.

God had brought us through. We were in good health in spite of the inadequacy of the camp diet. The Red Cross had helped to kit us out with some clothing on our way home by sea, we had kind relatives to go to, and our trust in God had been strengthened through being tested. The Lord graciously provided us with a house in the Kentish seaside town of Deal, where we could live as a family during 1946. In the internment camp, the Chefoo School staff had continued to teach us in the face of severe limitations of every kind. But now I had my first experience of school in England, when for three terms I travelled by train daily from Deal to Dover to attend the Dover County Grammar School for Girls. This was an ordeal to begin with, for the strangeness of everything chilled me.

In 1947 my father was appointed to become headmaster of the Chefoo School, which was to start up afresh, no longer in Chefoo but in Shanghai. For the first time our family was divided. Four of us embarked for the USA *en route* for China, leaving my brother in boarding-school in England. During that year the number of children in Chefoo School grew to over a hundred. I and another girl, at thirteen or fourteen, were the oldest of the lot. By a marvellous provision of God, at the end of 1947 the school was able to move out of its temporary premises in the city of Shanghai to unoccupied school buildings in Kuling, a summer resort in the mountains in the province of Jiangxi, more than 400 miles from the coast along the Yangtze River. Though we had loved the hills, beaches and sea at Chefoo, in Kuling we came to love the mountains, the rivers and rock pools, the adventurous paths and abundant vegetation. Our situation seemed remote from the mainstream of political affairs, but the radical change advancing upon the nation was to leave no corner of the land untouched.

On 1 October 1949, the People's Republic of China was born; Chairman Mao was supreme. Later that month I sat my School Certificate exams, the exam papers having only just arrived from England. At the end of the year my parents and I travelled to Shanghai. I was bound for England where I would complete my final two years of secondary schooling. We said goodbye on 6 January 1950. They returned to Kuling, and I stayed on my own in the headquarters of the CIM, which houses a large number of missionaries in transit or living there permanently. I had recently turned sixteen. The months went by and no ships could enter the port on account of mines laid in the mouth of the river. Eventually I was put on a train bound for the northern port of Tientsin, and from there I sailed to Hong Kong. My escort was an elderly CIM woman returning to the UK to retire. Together we set out from Hong Kong on the long sea voyage to England.

Arrangements had been made for me to stay with an uncle and aunt who lived near Bedford, and to attend the high school. The summer term was well advanced when I entered the Lower Sixth form.

One afternoon in July I cycled home from school to be told that a telegram had arrived from my mother in Kuling. My father, at the age of almost fifty, had died of a cerebral haemorrhage while playing a game of tennis. I was desolate. The foundations of my world were shaken. Even my brother, sharing in the same grief, seemed a stranger, as we had not seen each other for over three years. I know the Lord was sheltering me with his arms of love in the midst of my devastation when I had no close friend at hand. I also know that there were people in China and in England praying for us. In the spring of the following year, my mother and sister left China in the great exodus of missionaries brought on by the Communist government's hostility to Christianity and to foreigners.

Later in 1951, God guided an elderly servant of his to offer us a flat in his home in Bedford. My brother was a student in Cambridge and then in Bristol; my sister and I both went to the high school in Bedford, and my mother bravely took up teaching in local village schools.

University education

After two years at the High School and passing my A-level exams, I embarked on a university career at Bedford College, London University, reading English. An intercollegiate series of lectures affected me most deeply. The lecturer opened a door for us into the world of *The Waste Land* and other poems by T. S. Eliot. Being a student and living in a hall of residence in Regent's Park in the heart of London was a privilege. My sheltered Christian upbringing, my feeling still a relative stranger to life in England, our family sorrow and loss, and my shyness and reserve coloured my university experience.

At school, friendships formed through my taking part in the small Christian Union were important. At university, as well as the privilege of good friends, I also had opportunities to study the Bible with others, and the chance to help in leading the life and witness of the Bedford College Christian Union. On Sundays some of us would walk to All Souls, Langham Place, where we benefited from the preaching of the rector, the Reverend John Stott. Two particular passages of Scripture belonging to my university years are Psalm 16:2: 'I said to the LORD, "You are my Lord; apart from you I have no good thing,"' and 2 Corinthians 5:15, 'And he died for all, that those who live should no longer live for themselves but for him who died for them and was raised again.'

When I went on to study for a postgraduate certificate in education at the Institute of Education in the University of London, I again joined the Christian Union. There I met a young woman from South Africa who had become a Christian as an adult. I envied her experience, thinking it to be preferable to mine in that I had no non-Christian past out of which I had been rescued. But as time went on, the Lord showed me the folly of such thinking by causing me to discover for myself that I am a sinner by nature, and to understand that Christ died in my place no less than in the place of those whose conversion produces in them a startling change, observable to the outsider.

Missionary training

I was now trained to be a teacher of English and ready to begin. I successfully applied for a teaching post in Bedford, the town where my mother continued to live. So I joined her in our home at the same time as joining the staff of Dame Alice Harpur School for Girls. It was a difficult initiation, partly because, once the headmistress knew my position as an evangelical, she would not allow me to teach Scripture, as well as English, though this was included in my job description. Instead I had to teach some history classes, without my having any previous knowledge of the subject matter. The result was painfully unsatisfactory.

Since I had first begun to set my face towards South America, I had not lost the sense that there lay my future. At Bedford High School, I had been able to begin learning Spanish. Timetable changes prevented me from continuing this for a second year, but I later came to appreciate what a good foundation my Spanish teacher, Miss Bartell, had given me in pronunciation, grammar and vocabulary. This was a gift from God, together with a love for the Spanish language which has persisted throughout my life.

In the first term of my second year of teaching I had my twenty-fourth birthday. For this occasion my mother gave me a card with a Bible reference on it: Proverbs 4:25–26: 'Let your eyes look straight ahead, fix your gaze directly before you. Make level paths for your feet and take only ways that are firm.' God used these words to convince me that I could not dismiss my childhood's dream of South America without disobeying what I now knew to be a call from him. I had no option but to 'look right on'. I gave in my notice that I would leave my post at the end of the school year, and in due course was accepted for missionary training at St Michael's House, Oxford. This was an Anglican establishment for the training of women as parish workers, teachers of religious knowledge in schools, or as missionaries. Forty of us from different walks of life made up the student body in the autumn of 1958 when I entered the college.

I had had no links with any missionary society working in South America before I started training. Providentially, through the generosity of an older Christian lady who knew me slightly,

I attended my first conference of the South American Missionary Society in early 1959. During the following year, I applied to become a member of SAMS. The selection committee asked if I was making an open offer, or if I had a specific field in mind. On hearing that my offer was open, they told me they thought I should go to Chile. My mother encouraged me to take this step, though it meant that a great distance would separate us for a long time, just as she encouraged my brother who left shortly after I had done, to serve the Lord in Kenya.[2] I departed by train from London on 29 September 1960 for Liverpool. A passenger ship, SS *Reina del Mar*, bound for Valparaiso, Chile, sailed that day with me on board. On 1 November we reached our destination after a fascinating voyage, stopping at many ports on our route across the Atlantic to the Caribbean, through the Panama Canal and down the Pacific coast of the continent of South America. Now I began to see for myself the land to which God had called me. In his great mercy, the sense of being called and sent by him remained with me through thick and thin over all the years that lay ahead.

Church allegiance

Both my grandfathers were ministers of the gospel who became clergymen of the Church of England. Hence both my parents were brought up in the Church of England. They joined an interdenominational missionary society. The staff and children of the Chefoo School came from a variety of Christian denominations, and the school services followed a nonconformist pattern.

In the city of Chefoo two English-speaking churches served the resident foreign community. One was Anglican with an English chaplain, and the other, called the Union Church, served the needs of the non-Anglicans. I was baptized as a baby in the Anglican church where, nearly three years before, my parents had been married. Every Sunday morning our family would walk along the Bund (the road that ran beside the sea) to the church, until we were removed from our home and taken into internment camp. Years later, at the age of seventeen, I was confirmed in St Alban's Abbey, when we were living in Bedford and attending St John's Church south of the river.

In my student days in London and Oxford I attended Anglican churches in both cities. As a member of SAMS in Chol Chol, southern Chile, and later in Santiago, the capital, I took part in the life of Anglican congregations founded by SAMS missionaries. For a period I was responsible for visiting the homes of some of the women members of the Santiago congregation who worked as maids.

As the student work expanded, I spent more time travelling out of Santiago. This gave me the priceless opportunity of visiting many congregations of different denominations where there were university students. In my final years in Santiago, the Anglican scene had undergone great change. I lived in an area of the city far from any Anglican congregation and within easy walking distance of the Iglesia Evangélica Pentecostal. Here I found my spiritual home for that time and have great cause to thank God for this unique opportunity. Through SAMS I became linked to six Anglican churches in England. They gave generously towards my support and prayed for me; I spent time visiting them when on home leave. On moving to La Paz, Bolivia, I was involved in the founding of the first Anglican congregation in the city. Later, a second congregation was begun in another district of La Paz and I took part in the life of this one to which I could walk from where I lived. At the time of writing, David and I belong to a Baptist Church in Hereford.

My ministry in Chile

Chile is a republic with a democratically elected president, senators and deputies, outward-looking, progressive and peace-loving. But when Salvador Allende was President, from 1970 to 1973, he steered the nation into an extremely turbulent transition towards socialism. His government terminated abruptly on 11 September 1973, on account of a military coup headed by General Augusto Pinochet. Both the three years of socialism and the following long period of military rule affected the universities and student life profoundly. Under the former, political ideology was more important than study; under the latter, independent thinking was discouraged and the goals became academic success, money and a comfortable life. Many private universities were founded in the 1970s and 1980s.

From 1960 to 1963 I was a member of staff of a new, small, rural, residential secondary school in the small town of Chol Chol, in southern Chile, situated between Temuco and the coast. During this period, Dr John White, then Regional Secretary of the IFES in Latin America, visited Chile, got in touch with me and shared the vision of the need for an evangelical, interdenominational, student movement to be formed in Chile. Hesitantly and fearfully, though certain of God's leading, I told John I was willing to be involved in this pioneering venture.

It seems to me that my ministry was essentially one of teaching adults, mainly of student age, both individually and in groups; when I preached I spoke to a mixed age group of men and women. I taught Christian belief and life, using the Bible as my textbook. I also taught matters relating to the life of a student group and movement. This ministry necessarily involved me in much Bible study and preparation. I still possess a large number of notebooks which I filled with my own studies and the talks I gave. I used the Spanish Reina-Valera 1960 Bible the whole time, becoming very familiar with it. I found myself in a pioneering situation in both republics, as neither in Chile nor in Bolivia had there ever been an IFES-affiliated movement. In Chile exploratory contacts had been made prior to my arrival; in Bolivia there had been a student movement, AGUEB, in the 1960s and 1970s, which maintained fraternal relations with both Campus Crusade and the IFES, but remained independent. The fact of my being a pioneer meant that I was in a lonely situation. No SAMS colleague worked with me among the students in Chile, and only gradually were there Chileans coming up through the movement with whom the work could be shared. I battled with loneliness for years.

Friends in Chile – the Cortés family

Don Nazario Cortés, a hard-working and successful business-man, bought shoes wholesale and sold them to retailers. He would set off from his home in Santiago on a trip to towns in the north, his car filled with boxes of shoes. Left behind at home were his wife, Anita, and his five daughters. The seven of them formed a remarkable family.

Anita became a Christian as a young woman about the time she got married. She too was hard-working and intelligent, having had little formal education. She taught herself to make clothes for girls using a sewing machine. With tears she would pray to the Lord to teach her as she struggled to master the craft of dressmaking.

Anita belonged to a Pentecostal church. Her husband was not a believer, but she valiantly built a Christian home by faith, prayer, example and instruction. Nazario came to respect her consistent Christian practices of kneeling to pray by the bedside, reading the Bible, saying grace before meals at the table, taking an active part in the life of the church, giving practical help and sympathy to those in need or distress, and offering hospitality to relatives and to brothers and sisters in Christ.

Nazario did not enter the church, but he would drive his wife to the services she regularly attended and then collect her at the end. Over the years his attitude softened; she won him by her patience, wisdom, kindness and prayers. Right at the end of his life he yielded himself to God before he died at the age of eighty.

I first met their eldest daughter as a student in the School of Economics in the University of Chile in Santiago, where I used to lead a small group in Bible study, gathered in a lecture room. There also I met the second daughter, studying administration. The two sisters joined the GBU group in Santiago, where they met students from a variety of denominational backgrounds, they having known up till then only the Pentecostal church and its practices.

In the course of time, the third sister entered university, to study social work, then the fourth, to study nursing; and finally the fifth, to study English. One by one the five threw themselves into the life and witness of the student group and took part in its leadership. One by one they entered their professions, married Christian husbands and had children.

The Cortéses' home became well known to the student group, for there was an open invitation to use it for celebrations or special gatherings. When IFES visitors came as speakers to the movement, they would stay there and be warmly welcomed. Anita was a superb cook and a most gracious and unassuming hostess. To me she became an older sister whose friendship and example I treasured. I was often an honoured guest at the family table. Once when I was sick they took me into their home and nursed me back to health.

Towards the end of my years in Bolivia, in August 1993, I heard that the five Cortés daughters were secretly preparing a great celebration to mark their parents' golden wedding anniversary, to which I was invited. To my great joy I was able to travel from La Paz to Santiago and to be present first at a service in the Pentecostal church and then at an evening meal in a restaurant.

Nazario died in Christ in February 1999. I continue to be in contact with other members of the family.

Ministry based in Santiago

In 1963 I moved from southern, rural Chile to Santiago. I flew to New York (my first flight) to attend the General Committee meeting of the IFES, held in Nyack, New York State. Afterwards, I attended a camp in Campus in the Woods, Ontario, Canada, and then visited several cities in Peru at the invitation of the IFES Peruvian movement, before returning to Chile and settling in Santiago. I worked with a small Anglican congregation, and at the same time made my first contacts with some Christian university students, known to Irma Eskuche, a Chilean friend, a research worker in the medical faculty of the university. For several months, Irma and I met once a week in the flat where she and her mother lived, to pray to the Lord for the work we believed he had committed to us to initiate.

A student group began to meet regularly in Santiago. During my first leave in the UK this group ceased to meet, so we had to start again, largely with the same students, on my return to Chile. I was now officially seconded by SAMS to IFES. In 1966 and 1967 I attended classes in the Department of Spanish of the Faculty of Education, University of Chile, Santiago. I moved out of a large building, owned by the Anglican Church and housing several missionary families, to a small flat which I shared with one other person. The student group made this apartment its base.

Growth of IFES in Chile

After I was seconded to IFES, I travelled extensively within Chile, north and south, to cities where there was at least one university and where we had contacts with Christian students. Sometimes I would stay for a longer period in order to give support to an emerging student group. Invariably I was given hospitality in people's homes. In 1975 the student movement, Grupos Bíblicos Universitarios de Chile, was officially affiliated to the IFES. This happened two years after the military coup headed by General Augusto Pinochet. Both those to whom I was responsible in Chile and I were aware that my work with the student movement would be completed once a Chilean General Secretary had been appointed. This took place with the appointment of Josué Fonseca in 1980, and I left Chile in 1981.

Josué Fonseca

Josué's home was in Talcahuano, an important port just north of the city of Concepción, some 500 kilometres south of Santiago, the Chilean capital. When we first met around 1970, he was a teenager, living with his parents, brothers and sisters. It was a Christian family, active members of a Baptist church. Josué's father worked in the steel industry. His mother, small and dynamic, was a leader among the women of her denomination at national level.

Josué was already a Christian when he entered the University of Concepción to study social work, travelling from home daily by bus. Josué's years at university were turbulent ones for the whole nation. Salvador Allende, the socialist president, was in power from 1970 to 1973 until he died in the military coup which ousted him. At the university, students were presented with two options, to be for or against socialism. The use of arms became common and study became secondary to political activism. Against this sweeping current, Josué stood firm for his Lord, linking up with the GBU group in the university from the start of his career and becoming a leader in it. He was fervent, impulsive, dedicated, persuasive and reliable.

After completing his five years at university, Josué moved to Santiago, in the early years of the military dictatorship which superseded socialism. Knowing he was called to be a pastor, he entered the Baptist Seminary. While he was there, two important things happened in his life. He met Erika, a fellow student, who later became his wife and the mother of his two children; and he became a part-time staff worker with the GBU in Santiago. This meant that he and I now became colleagues, and a warm friendship grew between us.

As the 1970s came to a close, it was time for me to move out of the student work in Chile. Having graduated from the seminary, Josué was solemnly set aside for this task and appointed the first General Secretary of Grupos Bíblicos Universitarios de Chile. I worked alongside him for a year until my departure from Chile in April 1981.

Josué (his name is 'Joshua' in English) was a lovely friend to have, true-hearted, warm, devoted to Christ and his kingdom, concerned for people, aware of larger issues than the immediate ones of the movement. He was quick, efficient and businesslike in tackling matters, and developed skills of teaching, preaching and pastoral care. I was very privileged to be his fellow worker and to leave the responsibility of the movement in his faithful hands when I departed for England and then Bolivia. He loved music, sport, food and laughter. Our times of prayer and Bible study together in the office were always precious.

Ministry in Bolivia

In Bolivia from the outset we were a team of three living in the same city: Marcelo Vargas (Bolivian), Maggie Anderson (a Scot) and I. Because IFES is interdenominational, the students I was in touch with, or wanted to meet initially, came from a large variety of ecclesiastical backgrounds, I visited many different churches, met many pastors, and observed many styles of worship, preaching and music, as well as being aware of differing doctrinal emphases. During my final period in Chile, I took part regularly in the life of the Iglesia Evangélica Pentecostal near my home. This proved to be a peculiarly enriching and heartwarming experience. In Chile my links with the Anglican church were strong in the beginning: in Chol Chol in the south and then in Santiago I had no other connections than with Anglican congregations. However, because of the nature of student work, my frequent travels, and my sense of being only on the fringe of the Anglican work then beginning among the middle-class people in Santiago, these links weakened as the years went by. At the time of my moving to La Paz, Bolivia, in 1982, SAMS and BCMS (as it was then called, now Crosslinks) had recently initiated a work there by sending a team of two married couples. Their aim was to begin an Anglican congregation from scratch in a middle-class residential district of the city. I joined this team, having been asked specifically to work with the Anglican church, as well as with students, once I had made the move to La Paz.

Another characteristic of my ministry was travelling. In Chile I travelled up and down the country by coach or train and occasionally by air if I was going to Arica, in the far north, or Punta Arenas, in the far south. I would be away for days and sometimes for weeks at a time. I also travelled a lot in Bolivia, but there were others with whom to share the work of visiting the student groups. In my latter years in Bolivia, I was invited to form part of the IFES regional team for Latin America, with a special responsibility in the area of teaching Bible study. Over the years I visited student groups or attended training courses in the following republics: Mexico, Guatemala, Nicaragua, Panamá, Dominican Republic, Columbia, Ecuador, Peru, Bolivia, Brazil, Uruguay, Paraguay, Argentina and Chile.

As a traveller in Chile, I received warm hospitality in the homes of Chilean Christian families. Somehow the opportunity to stay in people's homes in Bolivia was limited, I think because on the whole there were fewer Christian homes available, and people's means and space were restricted.

The IFES regional training courses were a very important factor in the formation of student leaders. They were important too for my own growth in the understanding of my task, of the Christian faith, and of the Latin American context. Working with students both in Chile and Bolivia, our aim was to encourage them in their witness in the universities, and to help them learn to take responsibility for their activities and to develop the qualities necessary for leadership. It was therefore a great joy to see this happen and to have a part in the process. Much patience and perseverance were required.

Lourdes Cordero: a Bolivian staff worker

When Lourdes and I first met, she was a student in the State University in La Paz. It was October 1980. I had flown in to the city for the first time, on a brief visit, my base still being Santiago, Chile. Not until several weeks later did I write the letters which committed me to moving from Chile to Bolivia to help pioneer the formation of a student movement in this country to which I had paid no attention until then.

Lourdes, however, knew that what I had in mind was the possibility of starting student work in La Paz. Though she did not voice the reaction she felt at the time until much later, the idea struck her then as impossible. Bolivia was in the grip of an unscrupulous military dictator. The university had repeatedly been closed for prolonged periods. Neither the time nor the place was right for expecting Christian students to catch a vision of establishing a witness in such a world of chaos and tyranny.

This unpromising initial contact with Lourdes was nevertheless the first step towards the friendship which grew between us over the following years, and towards Lourdes' total involvement in the life of the movement that came to birth in September 1982, when God's time was ripe.

Lourdes is small and uses a stick for her lameness, which she bears, alongside another physical infirmity, with patience and courage. She lives in the family home with her parents, in whose lives she has seen the Lord at work slowly and surely, through illness and adversity.

The times we spent together were mainly in the office of the student movement. We would meet for prayer and Bible study, dear to us both, and to talk about matters concerning students and the progress of the group. Sometimes I went to her house, on the other side of La Paz, and when we had editorial work to do together, she would come to my flat, where we would work uninterruptedly, seated at a small square table just the right size for laying out our papers and books on. Several times we went on holiday together and frequently took part in the same student camps and training conferences, travelling on long-distance buses, mainly in the rugged mountains of western Bolivia.

On one occasion we travelled together by bus to the small town of Copacabana where her family has a small house in which we stayed. The town stands on the shores of Lake Titicaca, a most magnificent sight in any mood and on any day of the year. But Copacabana attracts visitors for another reason. An imposingly large Roman Catholic church there houses an image known as 'the Virgin of Copacabana'. Drivers of buses, taxis and private cars take their vehicles there to have them blessed by a priest and then festoon them with confetti and balloons for the return journey.

Lourdes, born and brought up in La Paz, was accustomed to

its altitude of 13,000 feet above sea level, its hilly topography, its street markets, countless buses and taxis, its juxtaposition of poverty and wealth, modernity and tradition, its frequent demonstrations of social unrest, its spectacles of rhythm, music, colour and dancing troupes drawing crowds on to the streets for annual religious festivals, its brilliant sunshine and cloudless blue winter skies, and sudden, torrential downpours in the summer months after Christmas.

Lourdes was the first Bolivian to become a staff worker with the movement, apart from Marcelo Vargas, one of the pioneers, who then went on to become the first General Secretary of the Comunidad Cristiana Universitaria (CCU), the Bolivian IFES movement. Later Lourdes moved from part-time student work into the newly established publishing house, Editorial Lámpara, closely linked to the movement.

In Lourdes I found a sister in Christ, a colleague, and a friend who helped me to discover and appreciate her people, her culture and her country.

Concerning being single and becoming married

'A man's steps are directed by the LORD. How then can anyone understand his own way?' (Prov. 20:24). This statement removes from us the final control of what happens in our lives, and, more explicitly, of what we ourselves decide and do, and places it firmly in the hands of the Lord. Even when we think we know what we're doing, and what is happening to us, our knowledge is only partial, and an understanding of our 'own way' is beyond us. This is the background to what I shall say on this subject.

As both David and I peer into the distant past, we become unmistakably aware of God's being at work on our behalf and preparing us for each other in our latter years. He had arrived as a young man in Chefoo in 1938, and, after six months of language study, taught for four terms at the school where my father also had worked. When David needed a home where he could be looked after while he recovered from a knee injury, it was our house to which my parents welcomed him, and where he got his first impressions, recorded in his diary, of me as a little girl of five. In 1941 he married his first wife, Jessie Moore, a member of the CIM as he was. For many years thereafter our paths crossed only occasionally. Yet if we thought of 'DBT' it was like recalling a good taste. He too cherished the fragrant memory he had of my father, whose friendship he regretted not having cultivated further. On her part, my mother[3] had grateful memories of being nursed by Jess in Chefoo. In 1981 I spent several months in the UK on home leave. It was a watershed in my life, for, having left Chile, my homeland for more than twenty years, I had committed myself to going to Bolivia to work with SAMS and the IFES. A Houghton family holiday in the spring included a brief visit to David and Jess in their home in Herefordshire. Out of this renewed contact came Jess's request to receive my prayer letters from then on. Though she and I did not correspond, she continued to pray for me until she died in November 1993.

David knew from my prayer letters that I was planning to retire from Bolivia in 1994. He was certain that I was the person whom he wanted to marry after Jess had gone to be with the Lord whom she loved. So when I had less than a year to go before I expected to pluck up my roots from Bolivia, David began to write to me. When I followed God's call to Chile, and years later, to Bolivia, I was not unaware that this step of obedience made marriage for me unlikely. Single men missionaries were a rarity where I was, and as time went on the possibility of marriage, but not the desire on my part, faded like the glow of the setting sun on evening clouds. I was also aware that the work among students to which I had dedicated myself would not have been open to me in the same way had I been responsible for caring for a husband and children. I could understand the wisdom of the Lord's dealings with me in this and was comforted. Yet I did not abandon the thought of marriage. I knew it wasn't true for me to say I had been called to the single life permanently. I spread all my thoughts, prayers and longings before the Lord, whenever I needed to, and earnestly looked for light from his Word. As God's time drew near to fulfil his purposes, clarity and faith were given me. If I were to marry, all that was necessary was one right man, who had made up his mind to marry, and to marry me and no-one else. This was not difficult for God.

In spite of this gracious preparation of me by God, David's letters exploded into my life like a bombshell, throwing me into an inner turmoil such as I had never known. All was confusion and fear. My prayer was being answered, yet I wanted to run away as far as I could go! For a whole month the storm raged. At different moments I opened my heart to two trusted Bolivian friends who would pray for me. At the end of four weeks, God gave me the answer. I was to say yes. David and I were unofficially engaged for several months before we met in Toronto in 1994, just over thirteen years since we had last met. Near there we became officially engaged. I returned to La Paz, packed up my belongings, dismantled my home, said goodbye to the dear and the familiar, and returned to the UK in mid-August. On 1 October we were married, and I moved from my sister's home in Essex to my husband's home in rural Herefordshire. David was approaching his eightieth birthday and I my sixty-first. 'Your path led through the sea, your way through the mighty waters, though your footprints were not seen' (Ps. 77:19).

Chapter 7

Emmy Gichinga

Vivienne introduces Emmy

In July 1999 I made my first visit to Nairobi, the capital of Kenya, for two weeks to interview Emmy Gichinga (née Matiti), the only woman in our group of eight whom I had never met. She was the first woman staff worker for the Fellowship of Christian Unions (FOCUS) and pioneered among students in East Africa. We enjoyed six interviews together. I appreciated visiting her home and church as well as meeting her husband, John. I was also able to spend a day with students and staff workers at the Kenya-Focus Centre.

General information on Kenya

Nairobi[1], the capital of Kenya, is just south of the equator, about 5,500 feet above sea level and nearly 500 kilometres from the coast and Mombasa, the country's second largest town. Nairobi's population is over 2 million while Mombasa's is about 1 million. The official languages are English and Swahili. The medium of instruction in schools and colleges is English. In a population of over 30 million (1995), the literacy rate is approximately 59%. Over half the population is under fifteen. Kenya has one of the fastest natural increases of population in the world, with an average of eight children for each family.

Kenya gained its independence from Britain in December 1963. Since then there has been a mainly one-party system. President Moi has been active in politics since 1954. After independence he became Vice-President and then in 1978 President. While in Nairobi I read *The Nation*, an English daily paper. Corruption in Government is one of its main themes. Corruption seemed widespread. The improvement seems to be that it is now discussed openly in the press. With a weak economy, unemployment is increasing.

Women are becoming more aware of their rights. Polygamy, abuse, abandonment, female circumcision and rape are serious issues. Different marriage laws apply to different communities. Christian marriage laws follow monogamy, as does civil law, but Muslims are allowed up to four wives, and Traditionalists are polygamous. Christian men sometimes decide to take another wife under Traditional laws. Divorce is increasing in the country and in the church. The Reverend John Gichinga, Emmy's husband, is the only clergyman on the presidentially appointed Standing Committee on Human Rights. I was interested to read an article in *The Nation* on Kenyan women who have been ordained.

As well as differences in religion there are tribal differences. The Kikuyu is the largest tribe in Kenya, living in central Kenya and around Nairobi. The Luhya is the second largest tribe. Tribes living in adjacent regions intermarried, but for a Kikuyu marrying a Luyha was marrying further afield. In 1978 there were few marriages between Kikuyu and Luyha, but there are more now. Kikuyu traders looked for land and jobs in Emmy's region, but there was not much mixing. As John is Kikuyu and

Emmy Luyha, they did not at first consider the possibility of marriage.

The growth of Christianity in East and Central Africa

In reviewing the situation in East and Central Africa up to 1960 the historian Elizabeth Isichei wrote, 'Here Christianity had made little impact by 1900, and even in Buganda and Madagascar, Christians were in a minority. By 1938, Christians formed 8% of the population of Kenya, 10% of that of Tanganyika, and 25% of Uganda, and the period of great expansion still lay in the future. Today, 60% of the people of Uganda and Kenya are Christians, as is a third of Tanzania's mainland population.'[2]

The East African Revival (1938 to 1960) made a deep and lasting impression on the Anglican, Presbyterian and Methodist churches. Legalism, disunity, materialism and personality clashes hindered continuing revival. As Emmy explained to me, the river was wide but lacked depth.

Nominalism is one of the major problems of the church today. Nairobi is 80% 'Christian' but only 12% attend church. Now, at the beginning of the twenty-first century, about 80% of the population is Christian. Next come Traditionalists. A small percentage are Muslims. However, Islam is growing in Kenya, mainly through marriage with non-Muslims who become Muslims. From Emmy's ten siblings her youngest sister and a brother became Muslims on marrying Muslims. Islam also spreads through the deliberate Muslim strategy of establishing medical facilities – hospitals and clinics – as well as educational institutions. The main concentration of Muslims is in the north of the country.

The Christian church seems generally unaware of the spread of Islam and does little to educate and prepare its members to relate to Muslims and share the gospel with them. A few agencies are doing this, but until many churches take up this challenge Islam is likely to spread in the country.

Emmy tells her story

Background and early history

I was born in the Kakamega District (now Vihiga) of western Kenya on 22 September 1950, being the oldest of eleven children, all from one mother. A brother before me died soon after he was born. I was supposed to be a boy, to replace him. My father always commented, 'I wish you were a boy.' I did not know whether this was a compliment or not, but I took it to mean that I must behave like boys and excel the way boys were supposed to excel, especially if they happened to be first-born.

My parents met in a teachers training college at Kaimosi. After my mother became pregnant she had to discontinue her training while my father completed his training as a primary-school teacher. My mother never got any other training, married young and remained a housewife for the rest of her life. Thus she was completely dependent on my father to provide her with everything. My mother was for me a negative model.

My parents grew up in a strong Quaker (Society of Friends) area. Various mission groups were responsible for certain areas of the country under a policy called 'comity of missions'. Quakers were fairly silent on salvation and emphasized good behaviour and acts. I recall that both sets of my grandparents were first-generation Christians in our home area. My maternal grandfather, Joseph, was a church elder. My paternal grandfather, Nyambara, was not a very committed Christian. In many ways he remained very traditional. I still remember him wearing his blanket as he was not too keen to put on modern clothes. Both my grandfathers died when I was very young, in 1957 and 1958 respectively.

I saw my grandmothers for a much longer time. Both of them died in the 1980s at the age of eighty-five. My maternal grandmother, Phoebe, was a very godly woman. She always started and ended any event with prayer. I admired her deeply. My paternal grandmother was an only child, brought up by relatives, as was her husband. Maybe it was this that led them to be very possessive of my father, almost treating him as their brother, not their child. This had many implications for the family. I remember my paternal grandmother as a very strong-willed woman who had everything under her control in her family. She mistreated grandfather to the extent of occasionally refusing to give him food. I would then sneak some to him from our house. Grandma Zipporah professed to be a Christian, but I was not impressed by her witness, although she knew how to read the Bible. Her favourite story, which she often read or told to us, was that of Esther. I knew about Queen Esther and her uncle Mordecai from as early as I can remember.

As a young girl I was encouraged by my mother to go to the church. So each week I attended Sunday school. We had wonderful teachers who taught us lovely choruses which I remember so vividly to this day. No-one ever explained to us the need for a personal commitment to the Lord Jesus Christ. All I knew at this early stage of my life was that good girls went to church. Father used to teach the church choir. A gifted musician, he owned the only guitar in the village. His gramophone drew many men of his age to our home to play the guitar, listen to records, and dance. Soon after, he bought a radio, the first in the whole area. He was the first villager to build a semi-permanent house roofed with iron sheets, and with whitewashed walls.

So I grew up in a modern home in the midst of a traditional setting. My father was the trendsetter. A very successful school-teacher, he became the first headmaster from our village and the surrounding area. More children were born to him. As the first-born in his family, he had to provide for his siblings, including educating them. His salary was therefore stretched between his nuclear family and his extended family. His ever-demanding mother kept pressing him to give her his entire salary so that she could give him what she considered adequate for his family's needs. Sometimes she would keep all the money until my mother would plead with her, begging her to give us some money to buy the basic essentials needed in our home. Even as a child, I thought my grandma was very mean.

My father started drinking alcohol. By the time I completed elementary school he was an advanced alcoholic. Many times he arrived home very drunk. Then it was wise to keep out of his way and just do as you were told.

By the standards of the day, we were a very privileged family, having produced the first teacher in the village. I was my father's favourite child, the 'son' he had wished for. I grew up knowing that, though I was a girl, I was supposed to excel in school and do as well as any boy. That faith invested in me fired me and encouraged me to study. It nurtured my desire for education. Very early in life I realized that education meant success, so I determined to do whatever it took to excel. I passed my first public examination in 1960 after four years of elementary school. This infamous examination had been designed by the colonial government to fail many Africans so that few would end up well-educated. Father was so proud of me that he took me for a trip to a nearby district where he was teaching to show me off to his colleagues. I was only ten years old, but was feeling so nice inside that I had passed an examination that those much older than me had failed. I moved on to upper primary school. I was always the top girl at the end of every term, only being 'beaten' by a few boys ahead of me. Though the youngest girl in the class, I was the cleverest. In the Kenya Preliminary Examination in 1964, I passed so well that I was selected to go to the prestigious Alliance Girls High School, 560 kilometres away from home.

Conversion and calling

I was fourteen when I left the village to attend school and to study with other clever girls from all over the country. I had few worldly goods, but I was determined to study hard and make it to the top. I was usually among the first girls in the class academically. Alliance Girls High School took students from various tribal groups and all the teachers were Christian missionaries. My eyes were opened to many things. I began to think nationally instead of tribally as I saw goodness in girls from other tribes. I learned a bit about urban life since the school was only fifteen kilometres from Nairobi. I participated in many activities, including debating, drama, sports, the Christian Union and Bible study. During my second year at Alliance I committed my life to the Lord Jesus as my Saviour.

Vivienne continues

Morning and evening chapel services were compulsory, but Sunday evening was voluntary like the dormitory Bible study and the Christian Union meetings. Quite a number of the girls became Christians. Some invited Emmy to read leaflets and attend Bible study, but she was not keen to do so. In her second year she sometimes went to a Bible study as she had no visitors. Her peers were not so keen on religion. At one evening chapel service in November Emmy was converted through the reading of Matthew 7:21, 'Not every one who says to me, "Lord, Lord," will enter the kingdom of heaven, but only he who does the will of my Father who is in heaven.' The speaker talked about the brother of a friend who had been praying for seven years for salvation. Emmy started crying, feeling that she was bad and needed to change. She asked a girl who had been witnessing to her, 'How can I be saved?' The girl mentioned Revelation 3:20. Next day Emmy asked another fellow pupil, 'Why don't you lead me to Christ?' The following day she got hold of another girl and said, 'You must lead me to Christ now.' It was 5pm on 22 November 1976. God had sought her out and convicted her of her sin, and she became a Christian.

Knowing she was returning to her Quaker environment, where people did not talk about religion in the same way, her friends said that after her holidays she would no longer be a believer. She prayed, 'O God, help me to survive during the holidays.' When she told some at church that she had been saved, they said, 'If you talk like that, go to the Pentecostals.' So she prayed again, asking God to give her strength to remain a Christian. Then she felt a presence in the room and started speaking in tongues. After that she had great boldness. She said, 'I have become a Christian and I am going to remain one.' She grew in her faith by attending Christian meetings at school and becoming a regular Christian Union member.

At that time there were hardly any Kenyan women in full-time Christian work. She believed that God had saved her for a purpose. She faced challenges about her school fees as her father refused to pay them. Once she was tempted to suicide. She had very few possessions – one pair of shoes, one dress and her school uniform. She made her own clothes. Realizing the importance of education, she prayed for help to get as far as possible in her education. Then her uncles helped her with her fees, so she was able to finish high school. By then she was a school prefect.

Emmy takes up her story

In the school holidays, I attended youth camps to nurture my faith. I met young fellow Christians from all over the country, who encouraged me. I was determined to grow in the Lord. I also kept my primary focus of doing my very best in my academic work. I never wanted anything to sidetrack me from my goal. I feared anything that would interfere with my education and cause me to drop out as my mother had done. My role model was my mother's youngest sister, Auntie Roselyn, who had finished her schooling, done teacher training and was married. I wanted to be like her. During school holidays, I always wanted to go and stay with her: first, so that I could avoid seeing my drunken father, and secondly, because I knew she would buy me the personal effects I needed for school, and also give me some pocket money. I owe a lot to Auntie Roselyn and her husband, Wilfred.

When I completed high school, I was admitted to the University of Nairobi. While at university my gifts as a Christian leader were developed and for the first time utilized and recognized. Hitherto, I had been a very quiet, reticent Christian who was just a follower. At university, I became quite certain that the Lord was leading me into the leadership of the Christian Union. The Christian Union fell under PAFES (Pan-African Fellowship of Evangelical Students, founded in 1958), which later became FOCUS in East Africa. Through these links my association with the International Fellowship of Evangelical Students (IFES) began in 1972. Having grown up in an alcoholic, nominally Christian family, I had to look for Christian nurture outside home. My Christian brothers and sisters nurtured me, and became my new family. To this day fellow Christians mean more to me than my real blood relatives.

Vivienne on student work in East Africa

The English-speaking countries of East Africa are Kenya, Sudan, Uganda, Tanzania, Zambia and Zimbabwe. IFES historian Pete Lowman observed, 'With the growth of the evangelical student groups, something more suited to the local needs of the East African region was required, and so FOCUS was created. In time … individual national movements began to feel strong enough to affiliate to IFES on their own. This stage was reached in the late 1970s and early 1980s. The only FOCUS staff worker, Ahuma Adodoadji, soon found that with seventeen groups to cover in the region there was simply not time to be creative and go into depth with any group.'[3]

IFES staff worker Eila Helander, a graduate from Finland, joined him later in 1973. One of her objectives was to train an African successor. In 1975 her job was taken over by Emmy Matiti, who served with FOCUS as a staff worker until a year after her marriage to fellow staff worker John Gichinga in 1978. John, who succeeded Ahuma, was a far-sighted strategist, responsible for the East African work as the national movements came into being. Kenya affiliated to IFES in 1979 as the Fellowship of Christian Unions (FOCUS), and became known as FOCUS-Kenya.

Emmy's years with FOCUS, 1975–79

Having the opportunity to continue her education in the University of Nairobi, Emmy immediately joined the Christian Union and soon met Ahuma Adodoadji, the PAFES and IFES travelling secretary from Ghana. She strongly felt that she would be asked to become a CU Committee member – the only woman. She became Vice-President in her second year. Because she was independent and spoke her mind, she survived. The CU had a Sunday service worship sub-committee which arranged services in St Andrew's Church. Emmy was a member of the singing group. John Gichinga was also on this committee.

When Eila Helander came to meet with Ahuma Adodoadji, Emmy met her in the initial stages of her ministry and they grew to like each other. Eila lived in a small room in the university for a month and got to know Emmy. When she moved to a house, Emmy often visited. She became a model for Emmy with her simple lifestyle. Eila was helpful and adaptable, modelling Christian values in a cross-cultural situation. She was accessible as a mentor and friend, and was about four years older than Emmy. Then the Reverend John Stott conducted a university mission called 'The Dynamic Revolution'. On one occasion Emmy chaired and gained experience speaking in mixed meetings. The CU helped her to develop as a leader.

During Emmy's third year at university a small retreat near Nairobi was organized by George Kinoti, a Kenyan Professor of Zoology in the University of Nairobi, and the Reverend Gottfried Osei-Mensah, a West African from Ghana who was an assistant pastor at Nairobi Baptist Church in 1971. The retreat was designed for any Christian student who felt that God might be calling him or her into Christian work. Seven, including two women, attended. John Gichinga was present. All seven became Christian leaders. There Emmy clearly understood that she would become a full-time Christian worker. The question for her was – when? The leaders at the retreat had taught that when God calls, you do not have to be in a hurry. He opens doors. Emmy graduated and was posted to her former school to teach history and French. She was aware of God prompting her to be available.

Eila used to visit the Alliance School. She encouraged Emmy to consider becoming a travelling secretary. Emmy said, 'I am not the person.'

'I came to find a replacement', said Eila.

1973 was a difficult year for Emmy. Her father had been pronounced an alcoholic, and as the eldest she was helping to educate her siblings out of her university allowance. She wondered how she could manage if she joined FOCUS. She adopted a very simple lifestyle and learnt to save. She practically brought up her three-year-old youngest sister. Her oldest brother, who had been in prison four times, died leaving a widow with four children. Emmy helped with their education.

Finally, Eila persuaded her to pray and consider. Emmy was a member of the Executive Committee of PAFES so the women knew her. In August 1975 she resigned from teaching to become the first travelling secretary for FOCUS.

In August 1975 Emmy experienced her first IFES General Assembly, held at Schloss Mittersill in Austria. She also visited Poland, and the UK, where she stayed with Oliver Barclay and his family in the North London suburbs. This, together with attendance at the Universities and Colleges Christian Fellowship (UCCF) annual conference at Swanwick, proved to be an excellent orientation to IFES and UCCF. She was also more challenged to work with men as well as women, despite the bias against this. (At that time many believed that women should not teach men and most Christian Union leaders were men.)

While Eila was still around, she orientated Emmy. John Gichinga was the General Secretary and Elizabeth Gitei was the secretary and typist. Elizabeth is still working for FOCUS.

Eila left in January 1976. Other groups such as Navigators and Campus Crusade started working in the universities. FOCUS staff learnt how to work without overlap.

Emmy attended various meetings to get acquainted with Christian Union members in and around Nairobi – on the University of Nairobi main campus, the Medical School, the Kabete Campus, Kenyatta University College, Kenya Utalii where hotel workers are trained, Kenya Science Teachers College, Kenya Co-operative College and Egerton College in Njoro near Nakurie, about 200 kilometres from Nairobi. She visited the weekly meetings once a month and was eventually invited to speak and attend committee meetings. She developed her writing skills by producing a brochure about FOCUS and the magazine called *Life in Focus*. A literature sub-committee was also established. Her interest in literature led to the start of bookselling on a sale or return basis. Ten per cent of the profits were kept to finance a small lending library. She developed Bible study materials and worked on a booklet called *Christian Leaders*. Emmy took a special interest in women and women's leadership. She attended annual regional conferences and worked with Focus Associates (graduates). In 1976 she was able to buy a little Volkswagen. Driving at night was a challenge for which she especially sought God's protection. After Eila left, Emmy took over her house. Sometimes she stayed on campuses. Occasionally she spent a week at Egerton College.

She was a travelling secretary not just for Kenya but for East Africa. In 1975 she attended the Annual Regional Conference held in Dodoma, Tanzania. In 1976 and 1977 she made visits to the GBU of Madagascar, training leaders, and ministering to women. Solomon Andrea translated for her in that French-speaking area. She continued going annually to Tanzania to visit campuses in Dar es Salaam, Morogoro Campus, 150 kilometres from Dar es Salaam, and the medical campus as well as the Adhi Institute (agriculture), both near Dar es Salaam. She used to stay a week or more with the Reverend and Mrs Kadege and make day trips to the campuses. In Morogoro she stayed overnight on the campus, meeting the Christian Unions and staff, helping in training programmes and interacting personally with individual members. She also met the CU Patron and any Associates. Tanzania was conservative in its dress code. Women did not wear slacks. Kiswahili, the national language, was widely spoken. However, she was allowed to speak at Sunday services.

Emmy went once to Uganda. At that time the movement was not very developed. It was more conservative about the position of women. Emmy befriended the girls at a conference and corresponded with them. She met some of them when they came to Kenya. In 1977 Emmy paid her only visit to Malawi. The Christian student work there was very slow and Emmy teamed up with Hank and Cathy Pott from the USA and worked with individuals.

Marriage to John Gichinga

John came from a polygamist family. He is the son of the third wife – the seventh child in the family. His father took a second wife when his first wife stopped having children. The second wife had all girls, so he married a third wife so that he could have sons. And so John was born. Then the second wife gave birth to sons. In all there were seven sons and eleven daughters, but John was the first-born son. Emmy's and John's marriage was by their own choice, but they had to get permission from their respective families. To the Kikuyu, intermarriage with all tribes was approved with the exception of the Luo, who do not practise circumcision. Their marriage took place in Nairobi Baptist Church, but they also had a church ceremony in Emmy's home village of Ingidi, where gifts were given. Emmy's parents with about ten family members came to the Nairobi wedding. From John's side relatives could come easily, as they lived within an hour's drive of Nairobi. John and Emmy wanted to have their wedding in Nairobi so that many friends, especially from FOCUS, could easily attend.

A question arose about having a married couple on the FOCUS payroll. The IFES General Secretary, Chua Wee Hian, ruled that Emmy should be supported by her husband, so they received one salary. At that time 80% of the finances of FOCUS came from IFES and 20% from local sources. It was part of Emmy's work to encourage giving, especially among Associates. Even so, salaries were low and there was sometimes no money in the bank. After a year during which she suffered two miscarriages, Emmy resigned. She stayed at home until the beginning of 1980 and then went back to teaching. In 1981 their son was born, and in July 1983 Emmy stopped teaching and John left FOCUS to become a pastor of Nairobi Baptist Church. God guided Emmy to resign from her teaching job to work full-time as a pastor's wife. This affected her promotion and pension prospects. She backed up John in every way and was involved with the church newsletter. She helped structure a course for pastors' wives in two theological colleges – Nairobi International School of Theology (NIST) and Nairobi Evangelical Graduates School of Theology (NEGST). She also taught this course on 'The role of a pastor's wife' for two years in both colleges. For six years up to April 1989, Emmy continued working as a pastor's wife. The children went into primary school. Increasing financial expenses were a strain on one salary. Her father had died in 1980 and her mother could not understand how she could have resigned from a salaried teaching post. Emmy kept silent under the criticism and learnt to live on the barest minimum. She bought books at second-hand shops for the children. For about eighteen months God guided a woman in the church to give her a monthly gift of 1,000 Kenyan shillings; also a missionary who was leaving gave new clothes for the children. God provided through his servants. In this period she led both her children to Christ and bonded with each of them.

John and Emmy talk about their marriage

When John and Emmy had been married nearly nineteen years they candidly talked to journalist, Florence Machio, about their marriage.[4] By then John was a pastor of the Nairobi Baptist Church and Emmy was a professional counsellor and clinical psychologist.

John: We studied together at the University of Nairobi from 1971 to 1974, Emmy doing a BA in Education with a major in history and French, while I did likewise but majoring in religious studies and English. We were both members of the Christian Union. Romantic involvement probably never crossed our minds at that time. She was a Luhya and I was a Kikuyu – a difference we could not ignore. After graduation we taught in different schools. Then coincidentally and without consulting each other, we both got jobs with FOCUS/IFES, a movement that incorporated Christian Unions in colleges and universities in East and Central Africa. As General Secretary I worked with the men, while as travelling secretary Emmy worked with the women. We shared the same office for four years but did not really notice each other until after the third year. A close relationship developed and we got married in December 1978 after over a year of courtship. Some of the qualities that attracted me to Emmy included her independence and her ability to stand on her own feet. I discovered what a tender person she was and I think I was actually looking for that in my marriage partner. This aspect of Emmy's personality has really enriched our marriage.

Emmy and I have many similarities. We have the same academic qualifications in areas that are almost related. Our jobs involve dealing with people, especially their spiritual and psychological well-being. We are both committed Christians and love our independence. We are also both strong-willed people. Our major challenge came out of our similarities. For example, whereas I really admire my wife's independence and ability to stand on her own, I still expect her to fit into the traditional mode of a wife.

Emmy: I was attracted to John because he was interested in doing the same thing that I was – counselling. Also, he was handsome and good at his work. When John expects me to be the traditional wife, at times it proves difficult. I remember in 1983 I resigned from my job to be a full-time pastor's wife and for six years my life revolved round him. People used to refer to us as an ideal couple. I was always there supporting him – at weddings, funerals or any other function in the church. After our studies together in the USA the situation changed. As a full-time career woman again, I get home as tired as my husband. I am glad that John and I have an understanding on this. We both try to create time for each other but sometimes John gets so engrossed in counselling and helping other people and forgets that I also need to be looked after. We also realize that we have certain gifts and talents and must give each other freedom to utilize them. We are not in competition, but complement each other, and this enriches our lives. Our work entails keeping people's secrets, but once in a while, we consult each other and say, 'What would you do in a situation like this?' … Freedom and independence in a marriage are very helpful and these are the two main things that have kept us going in our marriage, plus the fact that I have John's backing and he has mine. John is more of an introvert while I am the opposite. It took us quite a while to adjust to that.

For better for worse … Emmy explains

I made up my mind that I would stick to this marriage come rain, come sunshine, and try to make the best out of it. My concept is that marriages are not perfect, but if they are just good enough this is something to cherish. Once the idea of opting out comes in a marriage, then either affairs or divorce might result.

Taking care of each other is our responsibility, says John

My marriage into Emmy's community did not face any opposition and I therefore cannot pinpoint that as a problem. She is a first-born in a family of eleven while I am the first-born son in a polygamous family. All our lives we have been used to taking care of others. For Emmy to allow me to take care of her is very difficult, in the sense that she is so used to being in charge and taking care of other people. Because of her upbringing and the role she has played in her family, Emmy is almost not willing to surrender that. What has helped us is sitting down and creating time to see what each one needs and thrashing problems out.

On handling money matters, Emmy has this to say

After growing in marriage one needs to feel independent. By giving each other this dignity, it does not mean that you should have either a separate or joint account. The dignity can be found only in the honesty and trust you cultivate in your marriage in the early years. John and I had a joint account from 1978 to 1990, after which we both decided to have separate accounts. This came about partly because I had started working again after the six-year period that I stayed at home. The trust we had in each other prompted us to open different accounts but at the same time retaining the previous one. But something happened seven years ago that really made me question my role as a partner in our home. I am a Luhya and we believe that the kitchen is the women's department and that nobody should tamper with it without the woman's permission. So it happened that John's uncle, who had stayed in Uganda for thirty years, came back home, and he did not have anywhere to live. John, together with my father-in-law and his step-brothers, sat down and discussed how they were going to help his uncle. We had a permanent house in which we had invested a lot of money, and another timber one. The timber one had two rooms and I was using one of the rooms as my kitchen. To help his uncle, John gave him the timber house without consulting me. I was only informed afterwards. I felt as though I did not belong in that home because my very own kitchen, which I am supposed to be in charge of, had been taken away from me. My position as a wife was in jeopardy, or so I thought. However, John and I were able to sit down and discuss the issue and resolve the matter amicably.

Balancing a career and children: Emmy talks of her experience

When we decided to go and study in the USA our son Mwema and daughter Rachel Wanjiru were nine and seven years old respectively. We took them with us, because they were still young. We enrolled them in schools in America although it was a bit expensive. It was a good experience for the whole family. Before that, I had stayed at home with them. As parents we had discussed the issue and we both felt that because he was very busy, at least they should have one parent to take care of them. Some people did not understand then why I had to sacrifice my career and stay at home, but looking back now I know it was worth it. When we come back from work we generally sit and talk with the children unless there is something that needs to be attended to urgently. They often tease us about our careers and we encourage them to choose their own careers and not to be influenced by us. When we quarrel sometimes and bang doors, we are able to calm down and tell them that mum and dad do disagree sometimes but that does not mean they don't love each other. By explaining to them the children are able to feel secure.

Vivienne resumes the story

Crisis Pregnancy Ministries, Kenya

Youth for Christ International, USA, sent Barbara Hammond from the USA to work under the Christian Action Council to Kenya to establish a centre to cover the issue of abortion. The YFC Director for Africa, Sam Aciemo, a Ghanian, lived in Nairobi, was an elder at Nairobi Baptist Church, and knew Emmy. Barbara and Sam looked for a Kenyan to be involved in this work. In April 1989 Emmy accepted their invitation as both children were now full-time at school. Emmy had been praying for money or a job so this seemed the answer. She had been involved in Nairobi Baptist Church work full-time with no reimbursement. She now became Counselling Director of Crisis Pregnancy Ministries on a very small salary. Using Barbara's two-bedroomed apartment for an office, Crisis Pregnancy Ministries, Kenya, started on 1 May 1989. The centre suggested five options for women dealing with such pregnancies: 1. Placing the child for adoption. 2. Getting married. 3. The woman's parents taking on the child. 4. Raising the child as a single mother. 5. Abortion. In the first month there were only four clients but the number gradually increased to eighteen. The ministry was publicized in newspapers, on the radio and TV and by leaflets. When Emmy left in August 1998 eighty to a hundred clients a month were coming.

In 1990 Emmy had leave to attend Wheaton College, USA, to do a Master's degree in clinical psychology. John also took a Master of Theology, a third of which was clinical psychology. They were classmates in some subjects. On her return in 1992 there was pressure to leave the job, although it was understood that she should return to it. The woman who had taken over while she was away gave her a hard time but eventually left and started a parallel set-up, taking documents and donors with her. Emmy's salary was increased and friends from the USA started supporting Emmy and other staff, while she worked at raising more local support. Interns came to do training in counselling. Volunteers were trained and training seminars were run twice a year. When other centres started, for example in Uganda, the founders came for about a week for the training seminar and to observe the work. Emmy also went for several weeks to Mauritius and Cape Town in South Africa to train volunteers. Now South Africa has several Crisis Pregnancy Centres. Emmy also went to Namibia to help start the work there. After nine years with Crisis Pregnancy Ministries, Kenya, Emmy decided to resign in August 1998. The organization is continuing and is still using Emmy's *Crisis Pregnancy Training Manual*.

Nairobi bomb blast

The Nairobi terrorist bomb blast occurred on 7 August 1998, killing 220 people and injuring about 5,000. A Christian Counsellors Coalition was set up and a disaster counselling programme introduced to help survivors and relatives. Three centres were established. Emmy was in charge of the Nairobi Baptist Church Centre which had ninety-seven counsellors with fourteen professional counsellors to supervise. Another centre was at All Saint's Cathedral and the third at St Andrew's Church (Presbyterian). The centres met together weekly and mobilized help and reached out to the families of those who were killed or wounded. Emmy wrote a brochure called *Trauma Counselling*. She was involved in this work until the end of December 1998.

GEM

Emmy was able to devote much more time to GEM, which she had founded in 1993. It was her own private counselling agency, called GEM Counselling Services (a registered body) of which she is the Director. GEM Counselling Services was registered in the country under the Business Names Act and Rule on 24 May 1993. From that date GEM was a recognized ministry to help people with emotional and psychological problems. She could not devote much time to developing it until her resignation from Crisis Pregnancy Ministries. GEM's motto is 'Aiming for wholeness and holiness' through providing individual, marital, family and group therapy for clients; performing personality testing and other psychological testing; maintaining good clinical records; providing consultancies and organizing special seminars for interested groups and institutions; writing, developing and publishing materials of psychological interest; and conducting and providing opportunities for research of a psychological nature.

For a while Emmy visited a blinded bomb-blast victim, who would talk only to her. This woman was pregnant at the time of the blast and now has a lovely baby. Emmy sees her at her home, but the rest of her clients come to her office. Besides GEM, Emmy is involved in a wide variety of other activities. She does some pastoral counselling in her home. She is Chair of the Kenya Counselling Association (KCA, a registered body). She is visiting lecturer at Daystar University for varied courses including 'Marriage counselling' and 'Basic counselling skills', and at the Amani Counselling and Training Institute. She is a trainer/facilitator for various organizations and institutions. She would like to do more writing, including an autobiography.[5]

FOCUS-Kenya

Since John and Emmy left FOCUS-Kenya, the work has continued and grown. In 1999 their Communications Director, Peterson Wang'ombe, listed some of the cross-cultural experiences in which FOCUS-Kenya has been involved.

1. Missiologists say that Kenya has twenty-six unreached people groups. FOCUS exposes its students and graduates to some of those people groups every year in an annual training mission that usually lasts about three weeks ... We also seek the partnership of local churches who later do the follow-up of the new Christians ... This year, we shall go to Marsabit, a town in the Northern part of Kenya. We were there ten years ago. One of the people who became a believer is now a pastor and has invited us to go back.
2. Through IFES, FOCUS sent a missionary to the Student Christian Movement (SCM), the then black student movement in South Africa in 1995 ... He's still there.

3. Similarly, FOCUS has a missionary in Tanzania who is helping our sister movement, the Tanzanian Fellowship of Evangelical Students (TAFES) especially in the area of Bible studies.

4. For some years, FOCUS gave financial support to a staff worker in EVASUE, the Ethiopian student movement.

5. During some of our conferences, we have sought the involvement of students in neighbouring countries including Sudan, Ethiopia, Eritrea, Tanzania, Uganda and South Africa.

6. Our triennial Commission conferences (mission conventions) have been especially used by God in raising mission awareness among Kenyans but also in our neighbouring countries. Sheepfold Ministries, a local mission agency that works among Muslim peoples in Kenya, was born as a result of Commission '88. The current General Secretary and Council Chairman of the student movement in Eritrea received their call when they were student delegates in one of the Commission conferences.

So, through faithful pioneers like Emmy and John, small seeds have produced big trees.

Chapter 8

Ada Lum

Vivienne introduces Ada

Ada and I had brief encounters at the 'Manchester 83' (UK) International Missionary Conference and at the IFES General Committees in Columbia in 1983, when we shared a room, at Ashburnham in the UK in 1987, and in Wheaton, USA, in 1991, at the IFES World Assembly. I also interviewed her twice in her home city of Honolulu, USA, in August 1999. We enjoyed some meals together and she kindly took a few of us to see some of the island of Oahu and for a picnic. We exchange emails and enjoy our opportunities for interaction. We used her booklet entitled *Luke: New Hope, New Joy: 26 Studies in 2 Parts for Individuals or Groups*[1] for many weeks in my home in Paphos, Cyprus, where I lead a church Bible study group.

Ada is probably one of the longest-serving and most widely travelled of IFES staff. A Hawaiian Chinese, Ada Lum joined the International Fellowship of Evangelical Students in Hong Kong in 1962. Her itinerant East Asian ministry lasted from 1968 to 1977, after which she became IFES Bible Study

Secretary, a role which took her to all continents, training students and leaders. On 3 May 1998 Ada emailed me: 'For myself I am pulling back on travel, mainly because I want to concentrate on creating workbooks for the classes I teach at the Bible Institute of Hawaii and because the present generation has taken over the Bible training we did in the pioneering days – howbeit in other ways!' However, she still does some travelling. So let us see how the long pilgrimage started and progressed.

Ada tells her story

Family and early life

As a child I hated 'living below King Street' – in the industrial area, peopled by immigrants from all over Asia and Europe, three blocks from the prison. My schoolmates all lived on Alewa Heights or at least above King Street. I was embarrassed that my parents were immigrants (from China), and especially that my quiet and gentle mother could not speak English. I wished my typically Chinese parents were as well-educated and sophisticated as my schoolmates' parents. On special occasions mother would burn incense to ancestors on the back porch: for example, on the death of their fourth child, who was the first son. This was a very traumatic experience. Three more girls and two boys followed. Growing up in a large family was a very strong influence on my life. I hated working in Papa's steamy guava jelly factory before and after school, while I knew my friends were taking piano and ballet lessons. I used to dream of the luxury of being in a family of two or three children, not ten. With every new baby there was a shift of bed space. Sometimes it meant three of us on a double bed. Sometimes it meant sleeping on the floor of the living-room.

Papa and Mama had no formal religion. Papa was a typical Confucian – honour emperor, ancestors and parents, and all will be well. He was a fine Chinese scholar, so he considered the Bible quite a good book. He left it to Mama to carry on the traditional honouring of ancestors. She periodically burnt joss sticks and offered bowls of food, while chanting prayers at a makeshift altar on the back porch. They did not require us children to participate in these rituals, nor did they attend any of the local Buddhist or Taoist temples.

Pictures of colourful western meals made me wish we had them instead of the simple fish and vegetables with rice Mama cooked between her hours of factory work. I dreaded cold and rainy days, because it meant that Papa would take us to school on his old, beat-up truck. I would have preferred walking the mile and a half, especially when he pulled alongside the shiny modern sedans in front of the school. We were bundled up in dark, heavy-knit cardigans that my parents had brought from China while our schoolmates had lovely, soft pastel sweaters. I wished I could have new clothes, instead of hand-me-downs. My younger siblings say they never felt these negative things that I (a middle child) felt. All this was surely the perversity of my childish envy of 'the rich kids'. It gave me an inferiority complex. But thank God I did not turn out a neurotic, culturally deprived teenager. For I also have strong memories of industrious parents who sacrificed for us and lots-of-talk suppers around the crowded round table that Papa had made. (He built most of the furniture, as well as the house.) In spite of our seemingly round-the-clock work at the factory, we had time to play. Together we made our own toys and created games at the riverside or on the streets – in the days when cars were not common in our area. Papa and Mama read in their spare moments, especially the Chinese newspapers and any other reading material they could afford. All their children have always loved reading good literature.

When I was nine, a new family moved into the corner house across from us. They invited us to church with them. My parents trusted them and allowed us children to go. I liked 'church' because the people were pleasant and friendly – and because it was more fun than staying at home. A year or so later a family crisis exploded. Our eldest sister at the university was dating – and worse, the man was not Chinese. To our parents this was shameful – immoral. For the first time I felt a loss of security. I took the Bible the church had given me and 'happened' to open it at John 14. Jesus became real to me as I read how he comforted his questioning disciples. He sounded very under-standing, patient and certain. By the time I got to verse 27, I was hooked. Since then, though I have fallen flat on my face time after time, I have never wanted to turn my back to him.

This first personal encounter with Jesus through the Scriptures was a seed planted in my heart. I became increasingly puzzled why more people, including church people, did not seem to know and love Jesus. The desire to tell others about him and his salvation grew until by fifteen I knew my life ambition was to spread his good news. In my third year at university I took a popular course, 'Inductive study of Mark's Gospel'. At last I had a practical and fascinating tool to use for introducing seekers to the Lord and for helping young Christians grow as disciples. And that's what God has given me to do happily for almost fifty years.

Mama was about seventy-three when she finally articulated her trust in Jesus. Papa had made a commitment to the Lord a few years earlier with the help of one of our church members. We had been praying for over thirty years. Papa was never as expressive as Mama in trusting the Lord, though she had always been a shy person, and he the more articulate one.

The elements in my childhood that I resented or found embarrassing God used years later when I began working in developing countries. During those early years of IFES, when fledgling student movements were popping up on all continents, there was only a handful to pioneer the evangelistic and leadership training. To take advantage of these itinerant opportunities I began to operate out of a suitcase rather than from a house somewhere. How I have thanked God again and again that he had prepared me to be ready to sleep anywhere, eat anything and work hard in any culture. Of course, I would have always liked a clean, comfortable bed in a private room. But working with students meant a lot of hard bunk beds at month-long leadership camps. Living situations between these camps often meant sleeping in the corner of a shared bedroom or living-room, or even a shared bed and sometimes very public bathrooms and toilets.

Besides God's practical preparations years before, two other facts helped me to adjust. First, my hosts were lovingly offering the best they had. Secondly, Jesus himself led a simple lifestyle. As he said, 'Foxes have holes and birds of the air have nests, but the Son of Man has nowhere to lay his head' (Luke 9:58).

That was the physical side. As important were the cultural, religious, generational factors. About 98% of the students we worked with were the first generation to get a university education in their families. When I visited their homes, I could quickly understand the growing knowledge and cultural gap between them and their parents. Moreover, many of them were the first Christians in their pagan families. In those tensions I could deeply empathize with the new generation.

Vivienne describes Ada's ministry

Ada found her Chinese race a help in her travels. In the mid-1960s she recalled being caught up in student protests in Vietnam, Korea and the Philippines. In Vietnamese clothes, she looked Vietnamese. She was advised to keep silent before the Viet Cong. Once in 1965 the bus broke down in the dark in the middle of Viet Cong territory. Passing cars picked up over fifty passengers for a price until only Ada and her translator were left. A passing car came and they had to hand over all the money they had in exchange for a lift to the next town. Sometimes she did not know she was in danger until afterwards. In 1969 Ada wrote from Indonesia, 'When I landed in Djakarta last week the immigration official addressed me in Indonesian! ... But as in other Asian countries it is convenient to melt inconspicuously into the national crowd.

'All of this has not been heroic on my part. Living out of a suitcase on different continents has not always been easy. If there were things I gave up, it was only to learn later that the sacrificial exchange was dropping the pebbles for diamonds. For I began to feel rich, very rich in stretching my creative powers and learning deeply about my common humanity with others. It has been Jesus' way for me to work out my discipleship under his loving lordship. I wouldn't exchange these years for a million dollars. If I had not obeyed our Lord in these great adventures for his kingdom, he would have raised up others to do the job (and he has), but I would have been the loser.'

An itinerant ministry

The blurb to Ada's book *A Hitch-hiker's Guide to Mission*, published in the USA and UK,[2] gives a pen-portrait of the writer. Ada declared, 'I never had any intention to write books.' 'For many years, Ada Lum's job whisked her around Asia with her baby-typewriter, her entire home and office in one suitcase. She discovered that mission means both the making of disciples and encounters across cultures. She had originally expected to go to China. Much to her surprise, Ada ended up on an adventure that would take her from Hawaii to Hong Kong to Pakistan to Brazil to London and back to Hawaii again.'

Ada spoke of her work with IFES. 'Neither IFES nor I had planned that I would have an itinerant ministry after my first assignment. Never in my wildest imagination could I have conjured up such an idea for a woman. In fact, like any woman, what I most wanted was to settle down into my own home and minister out of it, not out of a suitcase. I wanted the security of a five-year plan. I wanted to study at a spacious desk with a library at hand. Under these conditions I would happily serve the Lord. But that was not to be. Those were the years when God was establishing evangelistic student movements in every Asian country where it was politically possible. He was raising up his leaders everywhere for a new age in his churches in Asia, and they were calling for whatever help we could give them. No, IFES had no five-year plan for me, but it did have David Adeney, who was then the associate General Secretary for East Asia. We were two of only three staff workers for Asia. David was advance party and seed sower in new countries, trouble-shooter and counsellor in emerging movements – a true Barnabas. When, in our travels, we could meet at an airport or city, he would always be ready with three or four possible assignments. Like his namesake, David was truly 'a man after God's own heart'. I usually trusted his judgments and always he listened to my side of the story. For pioneering work, a relationship with such an experienced partner is far more important than a five-year plan. Some friends think that living out of a suitcase must have been a great sacrifice for me. There have been struggles, but in my heart of hearts I had always wanted a simple lifestyle – not to be encumbered with unnecessary possessions. The Lord did not force the itinerant lifestyle on me for the sake of his work. Choice of a ministry is prior to choice of a lifestyle.'[3]

In 1976 at the age of fifty Ada wrote a booklet on singleness called *Single and Human.*[4] Let two quotations suffice. 'There is nothing inherent in any marital status to make one more spiritual than another. Singleness provides opportunities for growing into a mature person. Marriage provides opportunities for growing into a mature person. One can grow hard and bitter as a single person. One can grow hard and bitter as a married person. I know sour old maids and sour old marrieds. I know some beautiful marriages that make me wish I could be married like that. But I also know unmarried women and men whose lives are more fulfilled than many married people's. It is not because they are single. I believe it is because by God's grace they are taking their discipleship seriously under Christ's personal tutelage.'[5] 'God doesn't intend in the slightest for us singles to live second-rate lives. Neither does he intend that our lives should be lived out simply as dull reflections of some kind of sublimated, compensating life. If we are living life God's way, we are living in the very best way that he has lovingly planned for us all along (Mark 10:29–31).'[6]

The importance of training

When I interviewed Ada in Hawaii in 1999 I asked her about danger. She particularly mentioned Vietnam in the mid-1960s. After spending extended periods there, she returned each year for the Vietnam leadership conference, as things were not going well. The experience in Vietnam shaped her ministry. She used to ask herself, 'If this is the last time that I am going, what should I stress?' The answer was that she should teach the students how to feed themselves. They were not allowed to meet together in groups larger than four in each. They kept on witnessing through small groups. In this way Ada began to develop evangelistic training courses for use in various parts of the world. In 1997 she returned to Vietnam for the first time after twenty-five years. One of the original seven, Phan Thi Son, who had graduated from the London Bible College, pulled out a yellow sheaf of papers and said, 'This is what you gave us in 1963, and essentially we still use it.' She was able to give a copy of a revised version of *How to Study the Bible*. Another, Cuong, imprisoned for eight years, was in Hawaii recently. He is now the President of the Vietnamese Theological College and Seminary in California, USA.

Excerpts from Ada's letters

Mid-December 1972 from Karachi, Pakistan

'These past three months have been full of rich surprises, like magnificent sunrises from a flat rooftop before Karachi awakens … sunny, coolness … the ancient culture of the Indus Valley … the feeling of being in Jesus' country in the Sindh Desert … And growing surprises like renewing fellowship and discovering a companionship with Chun Chae Ok, my Korean hostess on the PFES staff … living in a consciously Muslim society … watching people sparkle like a happy cluster of Christmas lights when they themselves make discoveries about Jesus Christ in the Bible study/evangelism workshops …

'At another staff meeting in Bangkok Andrew Way said, "What we need in Thailand is teaching not in systematic theology (usually imported from the West, anyway) but in biblical theology." This focused for me the crying need in the young churches in both East and West Asia for Christian thinkers, Bible expositors and godly leaders with shepherd hearts.'

Mid-September 1973 from Hawaii, USA

'Now I am zig-zagging between Canada and the USA, meeting more realistic Christians, intent on being an active part of God's world mission. They keep asking, "Where can we serve?" I keep answering, "The place isn't important. Learn to be more vigorous in your discipleship now. Be bolder in your evangelism. Develop the gifts God has given you, especially the gift of opening up the Scriptures for others to understand. Keep praying for God's people and their ministries. Then he'll show the 'where'."'

Looking back in 1973: continued growth, 'like apostolic times'

In October 1973 Ada wrote from Hawaii, USA: 'Looking back

over the last three to four years in Asia, I realize what a rich life I've had in fellowship with brothers and sisters in its thirteen evangelical student movements sweeping southward from Korea to Indonesia and then westward to Pakistan ... God has been especially active evangelistically among the Korean and Taiwanese movements which have been absorbing thousands of new converts. He has been expanding the literature programmes of countries like Japan, the Philippines and Hong Kong ... These same movements have also been the earliest to produce full-time Christian workers and missionaries. God has kept the Vietnamese IVCF through the dreadful war years with and without national staff. During this past year a graduate returned from theological studies abroad to serve Christ among the students again. God has raised up a pioneering student movement in vast Indonesia ... Two national workers and their faithful, able wives are overworked, but they are rejoicing to see students turn to the Lord. He has brought strong leadership to Singapore and Malaysia ... He has kept track of the seven students in the first leadership training camp of the Thai Christian students in 1970 ... One has become the first Thai staff, two have just begun their theological studies abroad. The others are helping to form a Teachers Christian Fellowship and a Graduates Christian Fellowship. God is rewarding the faithful sacrificial ministry of our Indian brothers and sisters ... Staff workers are reporting unprecented interest and conversions among the Hindus in their conferences and Bible studies. In Pakistan God has brought together a staff team of Pakistani graduates under Mr B. U. Khokhar, an experienced man of God.

'It sounds like apostolic times. We seem to be living amidst the Acts of the Asian Apostles. We greatly rejoice. But like the first-century church we also have real, earthy problems, constant political upheavals, government corruption and demoralization that upset plans and progress, leadership crisis in the transitions from first-generation pioneers to second- and third-generation consolidators, both on the staff and student levels, superficial discipleship, respectability of the movement … If I were to cite one major, on-going need, it would be for apostolic dig-ins. I am impressed that Paul and his co-workers deliberately dug in for a year or two or three for a teaching ministry, not only for a select few but for the whole church.'

Further growth in the mid-1970s

'I wonder what God has in store for us in Thailand … (That's where "Asia's most docile students" toppled a long-entrenched and corrupt military regime.) I leave this week for Bangkok. During the pioneer period of the Thai Christian Students I used to hold my breath every time I deplaned for a visit, for I never knew what new problem was besieging the tiny nucleus of seven or eight committed but fragilely young believers. God kept his hand on those babes in the Thai woods. Each has remained loyal to him in growing witness and healthy leadership. The TCS formed a central committee to help give national guidance to the expanding movement, which now supports itself and is about to take on a second staff. Pray for Prasarn, the first staff worker, Dr Theo Srinivasagam, an Indian missionary who lives and works with Prasarn at the student centre, and myself as we go to the universities and high schools for training in campus evangelistic Bible studies and biblical leadership. In late July 1974 I will attend the International Congress on World Evangelization in Lausanne, Switzerland.

'Brazil's first Congressio Missionario in 1976 was a wonder to behold and experience. All over the Third World we are witnessing unprecedented, energetic missionary thrusts. Students are bolder and more responsible in evangelism. Leaders are leading. The Brazilian emphasis was quite different from western missionary conventions, which usually have scores of mission agencies ready to interview candidates … The Latins are vigorously searching for and pioneering in new models of mission and ministry. For instance, young, self-supporting professionals are teaming up to work and witness together in unevangelized areas.'

From 1978 based in Harrow, UK

By 1978, Ada was based in Harrow, UK, working for IFES as Bible Study Secretary. She wrote: 'Until I die I want to be involved with promoting a more sensitive and realistic international co-operation in this exciting global mission. During the past fifteen to twenty years God has been raising up indigenous student movements in every Asian country where it is politically possible. Now, our pioneering areas are elsewhere. A base in London makes it easier for us to train new staff, to go with them into the Muslim world, the Catholic countries of Europe and Latin America, as well as certain parts of Africa, and the Communist countries of East Europe.'

In 1978 Ada wrote from Harrow: 'Pray with us for unity of heart and for a spirit of expectancy to learn not only doctrine (fairly easy), but also to learn to think biblically (fairly difficult); not merely to learn skills, but to know more intimately the content of our message, Jesus Christ. Pray with us for courage to change and be changed.' Later that year she wrote, 'It is not our aim to build a large international team. Rather we are committed to working ourselves out of front-line positions as soon as it's biblically wise ... We know that we can err and have erred by leaving a pioneering work prematurely. How can we know the hour of departure? Is Jesus not our example of working intently while keeping close to the Father's heart so we can know when "the hour has come"?'

Ada called home to be based in Hawaii

In 1982 Ada wrote from Harrow, UK, 'On returning from East

Africa to England, the first thing I learned was that Mother in Hawaii has lung cancer ... The prognosis is not good, clinically speaking. She turns eighty-five in August and has other bodily complications. Happily for all, Mother is crystal clear that she is ready to "go early to the Father in heaven" and is grateful for a good long life. My brothers and sisters, who vary in spiritual clarity, have been warmly supportive, especially Ginny, who has constantly lived at home with our aging parents – with her bedroom door open each night. She has unstintingly and unflaggingly encouraged me in my overseas ministry, convinced of its strategic importance ... Years ago I told her that on the day she feels she can no longer take it alone, I would come home. That day has come.

'IFES knew of this possibility when I moved five years ago from pioneering work in Asia to an inter-continental work as Bible Study Secretary, based in England. So, though it was emotionally wrenching for me, together we came to some decisions rather quickly. I would be based immediately in Hawaii for my remaining time with IFES, reducing travel and catching up with writing and other postponed work. In mid-1983 I was appointed to serve on the IFES Executive Committee and afterwards I continued as associate staff for special assignments.'

Continued travels

After the death of her parents, Ada continued to work from Hawaii. In December 1991 she started to teach some classes at the Bible Institute of Hawaii (BIH). She wrote, 'I'm cutting back on long trips. But in 1992 I speak at several missionary conferences in the USA ... to challenge the next generation. Then in March I'm off to the Soviet Union and a couple of its former republics. In the summer, God willing, I'll return to my old stamping grounds of East Asia. In December I will participate in the South Africa IFES Regional Conference.'

In December 1995 Ada wrote from South East Asia, 'Sathien is a reputable surgeon, and Apiluck, a linguistics professor. Twenty-four years ago they were among five teenage leaders we worked with to get high-school evangelism off the ground. Today in their small suburban village they are helping to plant a church. It numbers about eighty after three years in very Buddhist Thailand. Would Paul have used Windows '95 and email to send his many pastoral letters all over the Roman Empire? What common sense and risks of faith guided Jesus' decisions in leadership training? Jesus of Nazareth and Paul of Tarsus have long been my models in mission and ministry. They inspire me to be flexible and modify for improvement … Certainly Jesus' progressive three-year training of the Twelve has shaped my preparations. Knowing that he was headed for death in his third year, he spent more and more time with that small group.'

In December 1996 Ada explained how her travel expenses were met

'Who pays for your plane fare when you undertake these training courses several times a year? Not BIH, but one of the following:

'1. The inviting movement. For example, Singapore, from which I have just returned, is an affluent country. FES not only paid for my round-trip fare. When they heard that the Philippines IVCF wanted help also in training trainers in Bible study but could not afford the Singapore–Manila ticket, FES generously paid that portion also. Great kingdom partnership!

'2. The inviting region. (IFES is divided into ten geographical regions.) For example, in March I will make my annual trek to Russia, this time to the Crimean region around the Black Sea. This pioneering area still needs outside help. So, the region will send me.

'3. A Sunday-school class with vision. For example, after eight weeks in Proverbs an adult class in Pearl City took up a "love offering for your next trip" to Vietnam. They spontaneously collected $845, the exact amount for ticket and visa.

'4. "Free" tickets from frequent-flyer milage. These serve very well for poorer countries that ask for help but can hardly pay their own staff. For example, I'll be able to return to French-speaking Africa for follow-up training.

'5. Card-carrying communist from Beijing … He attended one of my BIH classes. He later came to know the Lord when he was studying in Paris. He became a highly successful China consultant for a prestigious French bank, advising mainland Chinese on how to invest their money. We've managed to meet when I have been in Asia the last few years. We have good talks but he never asks about my ministry. Then last month in Singapore after a lovely mealtime, he stunned me by offering to host and finance a trip to Shanghai to speak to professors he knows. You can see that it's great having God as one's Financial Director. I think that's what Paul the apostle meant in Philippians 4:19. "My God will meet all your needs according to his glorious riches in Christ Jesus."'

Further travels

'The training sessions took place in a nation still reeling from a tribal massacre in which a million died and 700,000 children were left orphaned – and people yet unwilling or struggling to forgive "the other side". Never did I eat a meal in a home where there were not "added children". One young pastor said, "One day I have two children. The next day I have eight." Phocas Ngendahayo had invited me to train a new generation of Bible study leaders. All sixty previous ones had been killed in the war … Instead of fifty selected potential student leaders, 300 showed up the first day. Many of them probably came out of curiosity to see an "American lady". I'm sure they were expecting a tall, blue-eyed blonde, and not a shrunken Hawaiian Chinese old lady.'

Ada continued to travel in the BIH vacations. In 1999 she wrote: 'In July I'll join the quadrennial World Assembly of IFES in Korea (the first to be held in Asia). I'm no longer on staff, so I'm pleased to be invited ... Imagine the fun of seeing friends you have worked with in student evangelism on all continents during the last forty-five years. I am even more excited about the Bible Study Trainers Consultation preceding the World Assembly. Four of us presenters will show how we train students in Bible studies.'

In the 1990s Bible study trainers had to face some important changes in students. Ada described them as 'people who are wired for quick starts and snappy entertainment, who are not biblically literate nor used to thinking through any text'. In the Bible Study Trainers Consultation thirty-three representatives from twenty-seven countries participated in this 'crisis conference'. Ada wrote, 'Initially I was both relieved and worried ... I was encouraged, and now I am challenged. I was relieved to hear similar reports from nearly every participant. The climate for Bible studies in their countries is generally not good. So why was I relieved? Because I no longer felt alone. Global mass media in a postmodern world are producing an inter-continental culture where people read and reflect less and less.

'In *Sink or Swim in the New Millennium Culture*,[7] Leonard Sweet summarized contemporary values as: Experiential over rational; Participatory over representational; Image-based over word-based; Communal over individualistic (EPIC). Sailing between good humour and serious concern, he appeals to us who want to "do ministry" to accept these realities. Our contemporary world is not necessarily what it should be, but that's the way it is. He makes this provocative statement, "We may be seeing a time where God is more active in the world than in the church."

'I was worried because the reports of these colleagues shared similar problems and frustration in trying to help students to study the Bible. Christian students in our touchy-feely culture want to know God's Word – in the easiest way possible, and not necessarily from the printed page. The means must be entertaining, not taxing. Impressions must flow fast, not drag. Why study the Bible in a group of peers who are as biblically illiterate as you? Why not use increasingly cheaper videos done by professionals? They can communicate what to think and believe in far more interesting ways than students or even a staff worker ... Once when I commented to a student that it seemed his group was being constantly spoon-fed, he shot back, "What's wrong with that? That's better than not being fed at all."

'Why are inductive Bible study groups that were so productive at the beginning of IFES (and still are in pioneering situations) apparently ineffective today? It is my opinion that it's partly historical development. EPIC partly illustrates the perversity of our human nature – to take the path of least resistance and capitulate indiscriminately to trends – and partly our retaining the form of inductive Bible studies without Spirit-inspired content.

'Looking back I see more clearly than before why God raised up IFES in 1947 for the post-World War II era. Colonial empires were being dismantled. Nations were being reborn or newly born. Universities and other tertiary institutions began proliferating at a phenomenal rate to produce national leaders. The role of paternalistic missionary societies was severely challenged. Planet Earth was becoming a hi-tech global village.

'This gave opportunity to clarify our objectives. We are not discarding inductive Bible study but redefining it with new insights. Eric Miller, IFES Media Consultant, suggested renaming it "Interactive Bible Study". We need to consider other approaches that can enhance our basic teaching and learning of Scriptures. We must be sensitive and relevant, plugging into students' sockets. We have young leaders who deeply care about Bible studies.

'Among the BSTC participants were some "middle-aged" staff, chronologically between the young staff and myself. I had known them as student leaders and now as senior staff. At one point of my presentation Femi from Nigeria and Angelit from Peru burst out almost simultaneously, "You have changed!" Startled by their outburst I asked what they meant. They perceived that through the years I had evolved from a relatively strict inductivist to "a flexible interactivist". I had not been conscious of this evolution. But years of working with brothers and sisters in non-western cultures profoundly shaped my ministry. They taught me how to read the Bible in other than rational, historico-grammatico-analytical ways. Latin colleagues have enlightening cultural and psychological insights that I used to be wary of. Africans are great in dramatizing Jesus' parables, often expressing his humour that a solemn evangelical misses. Intuitive insights of Asians sharpen my perspective of God's Word.

'This BSTC, I had thought, would be my last global contribution. By the end of the World Assembly ten days later we had received a dozen invitations to help train young staff workers in personal Bible studies and in leading study groups. I look forward, God willing, to teaming up with training colleagues who have a passion for Bible studies. We must strive to be like the chosen ones of the tribe of Issachar, who "understood the times and knew what Israel should do" and inspired volunteers from their tribe to join battle with them "to make David king" (1 Chr. 12:32, 38).

'In his grand scheme of things God in the late 1940s and 1950s was raising up in North America a scattered group of people who were catching on to the inductive approach to Bible study. Many Europeans were already using this approach without labelling it as such. These young men and women had known only authoritarian Bible teaching. Says Jim B, "I was amazed to learn an independent way of knowing God's Word."

'This spontaneous movement gradually affected thousands of thinking young people and their churches in diverse cultures around the world. Inductive Bible study was the most effective tool of pioneering student missionaries. On every continent since the 1950s study groups were shooting up like mushrooms. These laid the foundation of indigenous national student movements linked to IFES. They number 150 today.'

IFES looking to the future

After the Bible Study Trainers Consultation (BSTC) in Korea, Ada Lum stayed for the IFES World Assembly. A thousand Korean Christians joined the delegates on 17 July 1999 for two keynote lectures. Dr Samuel Escobar's call to the Assembly enables us to see something of what the future of IFES may be. Among other things he said, 'Radical shifts in culture, politics and economics, as well as the growth of Christianity in the southern hemisphere, have brought new scenarios. Traditional mission models inherited from the Christendom mentality and the colonial era are now obsolete. It is time for a paradigm change that will come from a salutary return to the Word of God.'[8]

What Ada is doing now

'In June 2000 there was opportunity to teach at the Vietnamese Theological College in California. Dr Nguyen Huu Cuong, VTC's president, was our last IVCF staff worker in South Vietnam before the communists clapped him into prison for eight years. Another ex-student, now a pastor among refugees, said, "What? Is Elder Sister Adah Loom still living?" Maybe that's what other ex-students also asked before joining the reunions in Singapore, Malaysia and Thailand during August ... Malaysia's Fellowship of Evangelical Students hosted a regional Training Bible Study Trainers Course for thirty staff workers from these countries and the Philippines. Imagine what God can do through thirty motivated trainers in raising up hundreds of Bible study leaders among students back in their countries ... I had been told that this new Asian generation is as much affected by postmodern values as are young people in the West ... but these students turned out to be extraordinarily responsive (and fun-loving) to the course on "Keys to inductive Bible study". I've not seen such intense interest in the Bible among young people for a long time anywhere. They certainly put heart back into me for this postmodern generation.

'On my return to Hawaii someone asked, "Don't you find this local ministry dull after such excitement overseas?" Not at all! It's just as exciting teaching lay leaders coming to classes after a day's work, eager to know and serve God better by knowing his Word better. I wish you could meet them – old, new and not-yet Christians. They inspire me to prepare better and pray more.'

So, at seventy-three Ada Lum keeps on keeping on.

Epilogue

In these eight mini-biographies the theme of early or sudden death does not occur except in Gladys Peter's account of her daughter's death, and in my own recollections of Esther John. It is not of course always like that. It seems that all eight contributors are busy living out their full span. As my book developed it was suggested I add a little about Ellie Lau and Ruth Eldrenkamp, whose experience was very different. I never met them but I salute them and hasten to include their themes of sorrow 'surprised by joy'.

Ellie[1] was born and brought up in Hong Kong, the twelfth in a family of eleven brothers and two sisters. She was a kind, sensitive person, with a sense of humour, but a strong independent spirit. She left home to train and work as a medical microbiologist in North America. Then she served in jungle hospitals in Sarawak, East Malaysia. Her family had by then migrated to Canada. When God called her into full-time ministry she studied at the Discipleship Training Centre, founded by David Adeney and OMF in Singapore. After earning her certificate, she joined FES/Hong Kong for two years.

Although the different movements in South East Asia had become self-governing, self-supporting and self-training, an IFES staff member was still needed to help in discipling. Ellie, with her gifts of friendship and encouragement, was the ideal person to do this. She was also excellent in helping to promote world missions. So, in 1977, she joined IFES as the Regional Mission Secretary for IFES East Asia. For the next fourteen years, she travelled and worked in many different Asian countries, especially those with limited access to foreign Christians. She contacted those in student work: students, staff and staff families. Many people were encouraged by her fellowship. On her extensive travels she overcame cultural barriers by just being herself. She was not bound by conventions or rules, but was always enthusiastic for God's work. She challenged many students and graduates in East Asia 'to give up their small ambitions' for the joy of serving the Lord Jesus and his kingdom.

After contributing much of her life and work to Christ's church in East Asia, Ellie returned to Canada in 1991. A cancerous growth was discovered in her brain and nasal cavities. After a long period of living with the cancer, on 8 December 1997, aged fifty-one, she peacefully went to be with her Lord and Master, with a smile on her face. Many visited her during her years of illness. She was always an encourager and, by her patient endurance of suffering, influenced many.

The early death of those who seem to have so much to offer is part of the human condition. But what of sudden and violent death? Many Christian students and staff workers have been killed in revolutions, genocide, rebellions and senseless violence in their countries. Some have been martyred. Let one instance of senseless violence speak for all.

Ruth Eldrenkamp's husband Neal was murdered in front of her and their children. This is her testimony.

'Let me begin by sharing a couple of pictures. It's the World Assembly of 1991 in Wheaton, USA. My husband, Neal, and I were just starting out with IFES in Latin America. He tried out his timid Spanish with some questionnaires that would help direct our communications ministry in the region. Now it's the

World Assembly of 1995 in Nairobi. Our son, Jonathan, the only child in the Assembly, ran around greeting participants with a bright jambo.[2] His dad ran about filming, leading a workshop, interviewing people in Spanish and English. The celebration of our unity as God's people was boldly stated by the huge stage backdrop he had creatively constructed. He was thrilled to be back in Africa where he had served a couple of years during his youth. He was excited about our second child on her way. He was full of life and vision for God's work in our region. He yearned to share the whole gospel through the diverse means God has granted his people through word and image, light and sound.

'And now it's the World Assembly of 1999 in Seoul, Korea. I stand here alone. Jonathan, Luana and Natalia are back home in Buenos Aires; and Neal is in our eternal home, with our Lord. When he was shot to death almost two years ago by some car thieves, all the family dreams and ministry dreams were suddenly cut short. Life will never be the same. We have lost a loving companion, a playful father, a creative servant, a humble man of God.

'But why am I taking time out of the programme to share these things with you? The first reason I'm here is that I need to thank you, my family, for being means of grace to my children and me. Your love, prayers, gifts and words of encouragement have meant we couldn't crash down even if we had chosen to. They've been sustaining, as has been God's provision throughout my life through a God-fearing family, my church and the IFES movement. Second, I am here because I must witness to the kind of God we serve. He is the God of history, the sovereign Lord. Yet he has chosen to exercise his rule by giving his own Son, by taking upon himself the utmost pain of darkness and total separation and loss, consequences of our sin, so that we might live with him for ever … The third reason is that I must remind myself and others that this is the kind of world we live in: a broken world, full of emptiness, wracked by injustice and consequent poverty and violence. The question, then, is not "Why?" but "Why not?" Why should we as Christians expect immunity from pain and loss while most of the world suffers them? Lastly, and this is the main reason why I'm here with you today, is that brokenness is not the end of the story. Our pain is deep, but it is not all-encompassing; our loss is enormous, but it is not eternal; and death is our enemy but it does not have the final word. The wounded Lamb is also the Lion of Judah and one day he will reign in his perfect rule of love, peace and justice.'

Several other themes emerge from the accounts in this book. One is the way Islam is impacting the world. One would expect to learn from its presence as the majority in Pakistan, as did Vivienne and Chae Ok, or in Egypt, as did Rebecca. But Gladys was aware of it as a minority in India, which probably has more Muslim citizens than Bangladesh. Emmy illustrated how Islam is growing fast in Kenya, as it is in many parts of Africa, through intermarriage. Two of her siblings were converted to Islam through marriage. The lack of awareness of Islam and the ignorance about it in the churches in Kenya aids its increase from a small minority. Muslims have a plan and strategy for Africa which is being implemented. They have a mission to the world to make it Muslim. Tonica is well informed on Islam although few Muslims live in South America. She has been involved for some years in training Christians in South America, particulary in Brazil, in preparation for working in Muslim lands in the Middle East and Asia. With church renewal has come an increasing desire for information and training. Korea, like Brazil, is sending out many missionaries and tentmakers. In Chae Ok's chapter we see how Islam has taken root in her land which fifty years ago had no Korean Muslims. We also read of the Institute of Islamic Studies that she and others started in 1992, not just for Koreans but for those in surrounding countries, so that Christians might be well informed and equipped to introduce their Muslim friends to their friend Jesus Christ.

Another thread running through the book is the need of the poor, the handicapped and the marginalized. Tonica introduced us to José Gomes, a young Angolan who became tetraplegic during his teens through a diving accident. Chae Ok described how she was almost overwhelmed by the gulf between rich and poor in Pakistan. Rebecca, after meeting Salah, started to help in a whole new world among the garbage people of Cairo, of whom he is one. Later she also became involved in the same city with refugees from Sudan, who had fled persecution. The needs of Angola strike us all as seen though the eyes of Tonica. We might, in conclusion, ask how God sees his world, and what he would like us to do about it.

Notes

1. Vivienne Stacey

1. In 1974 IVF changed its name to Universities and Colleges Christian Fellowship (UCCF).
2. On receiving full independence from Britain in 1971 they were renamed the United Arab Emirates.
3. Later Archbishop of Melbourne.
4. London: Concordia, 1974.
5. London: Hodder and Stoughton, 1997.
6. London: Interserve, 1995.

2. Gladys Peter

1. See Pete Lowman, *The Day of his Power* (Leicester: IVP, 1983), pp. 149–154.
2. *Indian Missions* magazine, 1999.

4. Chun Chae Ok

1. See Vivienne Stacey, *Submitting to God: Introducing Islam* (London: Hodder and Stoughton, 1997), pp. 93–94.

6. Felicity Bentley-Taylor

1. Material supplied by Felicity.
2. My brother, Stephen Mosely Houghton, died in Nairobi, Kenya, in 1983 at the age of fifty-two.

3. My mother, Dorothy Blanche Houghton, died in 1990 in Tunbridge Wells, UK, at the age of eighty-five.

7. Emmy Gichinga

1. Nairobi is a Masai word meaning 'a place of cool waters'.
2. Elizabeth A. Isichei, *History of Christianity in Africa from Antiquity to the Present* (London: SPCK, 1995), p. 230.
3. Pete Lowman, *The Day of his Power* (Leicester: IVP, 1983), p. 256.
4. Published in the December 1997 issue of the magazine *Parents* in its series on 'Marriages that last', under the title 'Giving each other independence: the secret of our marriage'.
5. Some of Emmy's publications include: *Nairobi Baptist Church: Through 30 Years of Worship* (1989); and *Unmarried Mothers: A Counselling Guide and Basic Counselling Skills*.

8. Ada Lum

1. London: Scripture Union, 1992.
2. Leicester: Inter-Varsity Press, 1985.
3. Ibid., pp. 136–137.
4. *Single and Human: The Joys and Trials, Opportunities and Challenges of Being Single* (Downers Grove, IL: InterVarsity Press, 1976).
5. Ibid., p. 80.
6. Ibid., p. 81.
7. Zondervan, 1999.
8. Special report, Launch Issue, International Fellowship of Evangelical Students, 1999.

Epilogue

1. Ellie's colleagues Koichi Ohtawa, Goh Chee Leong and Ada Lum kindly supplied me with information and impressions.
2. An East African greeting in Swahili.